Laurie Boucke

INFANT POTTY BASICS

With or Without Diapers
... the Natural Way

WHITE
BOUCKE
PUBLISHING

LAFAYETTE, COLORADO

Library of Congress Cataloging-in-Publication Data

Boucke, Laurie.
    Infant potty basics : with or without diapers-- the natural way / Laurie Boucke.
    p. cm.
    Includes bibliographical references.
    ISBN 1-888580-25-9 (pbk.)
    1. Toilet training. I. Title.
 HQ770.5.B679 2003
 649'.62--dc21   2002155535

PO BOX 400, LAFAYETTE, CO 80026, USA

www.white-boucke.com

Contents

Preface

Pottying babies from birth or the early months of life? Most Westerners scoff at the very idea that an infant is able to work with trusted adults in this respect. Yet in much of the world, it is a fact of life and part of the bonding process. It is the most natural and instinctual way to handle the elimination functions and is an accepted part of the attachment parenting lifestyle in many societies.

The infant potty technique (IPT) is based on an elimination training approach used in much of Asia, rural Sub-Saharan Africa and South America. In this book, the technique has been adapted to a Western urban lifestyle in various ways, including the use of a sink, potty, toilet or other container; variations in elimination positions; part-time use of the technique; and, where desired, part-time use of diapers.

This book is my third work on infant elimination training. First came *Trickle Treat: Diaperless Infant Toilet Training Method* in 1991 (now out of print but available in many libraries). That book was written as a result of my own experience with infant toilet training and also was inspired by the fact that no other books existed on the topic. Next came *Infant Potty Training: A Gentle and Primeval Method Adapted to Modern Living* in 2000 and updated in 2002, a 500-page tome with extensive research, many long testimonials and a large selection of photos. And now we have *Infant Potty Basics: With or Without Diapers . . . the Natural Way* (2003), a book that combines attributes of the previous two works and includes some new research.

Why three books on IPT? The attitude of Western medicine has started to change. There is now disagreement with the widely held premises about maturational readiness for toilet training and the age at which babies can start to gain some sphincter control. At the same time, interest in this method has been steadily on the increase, and parents are hungry for detailed information on this nurturing method.

A variation of IPT was used in Western countries for roughly 50 years, until around 1950. From 1914-1945, the method was endorsed by the U.S. government in numerous editions of its publication *Infant Care*. Other agencies and experts recommended the same. Unfortunately, some of the practices were rather harsh and led to the conclusion that any form of early toilet learning is bad. For example, the method was based on the fixed timing of the mother or nurse, rather than on baby's natural elimination timing. There was little emphasis on baby's signals. Soap sticks (to stimulate BMs), punishment and coercion were sometimes used (These are all strict no-nos with IPT). After this came the permissiveness of Dr. Spock, the delayed toilet training or "waiting for baby to self-train" of Dr. Brazelton, theories on maturational readiness and the billion-dollar disposable diaper industry. These managed to not only completely eradicate IPT from Western thinking, but also to instill misunderstanding, fear and ridicule of IPT.

In 1975, Jean Liedloff's *The Continuum Concept* compared the child-rearing practices of modern, Western culture with those of the Yequana Indians living in the rainforests of Venezuela and started to swing the pendulum back to a more natural and instinctive means of child raising. The continuum concept emphasizes the importance of the "in-arms phase," whereby a mother or other caregiver is in constant physical contact with baby 24 hours a day (accomplished in part by using a baby carrier, preferably a sling), from birth until baby begins to crawl, usually around 6 months. At this point, the infant can leave and return at will to the caregiver. Liedloff maintains that Westerners are taught to disregard their instinctive feelings, which would support the in-arms phase, sleeping with baby, breastfeeding and being responsive to baby's cries. We have a natural yearning to be close to our babies but have been taught to ignore many of our parental instincts. We accept the notion that our babies can only grow up to be independent and unspoiled if we leave them alone and let them cry.

In the early 1980s, pediatrician William Sears coined a new term for the continuum concept and brought his own intuitive, high-touch and responsive parenting style to a wide audience. He called it "attachment parenting" (AP) and defined it as the five baby B's of bonding, breastfeeding, bed-sharing, baby-wearing and belief in baby's cries.

Interestingly, in societies where AP has been practiced for centuries, IPT has also been the norm. In this sense, I consider it to be a sixth Baby B (bladder and bowel awareness and communication) and hope that one day it will be recognized to be an integral part of AP.

Readers must bear in mind that each baby is unique and will develop at its own personal pace. Any parent or caregiver who desires to use this method with a healthy baby in a stable home environment, who implements it correctly and who exercises patience, dedication and diligence should be able to succeed.

Laurie Boucke
Lafayette, Colorado

Introduction

by Prof. Marten W. deVries, MD

Potty training is an important developmental milestone in all societies and therefore of universal interest to mothers and families. Cultures worldwide have given their signature to bowel and bladder training methods and back their approaches with specific ideas of what a baby is, can and should do.

Those who have studied and observed child-rearing practices across different cultural settings have been struck by the diversity of ideas, expectations and practices that guide parents and families in the day-to-day interactions with their babies and children. One observation by the influential anthropologist Caudill, who compared Japanese and American infant development and child-rearing practices during the 1950s and 1960s, has always loomed as a compelling wisdom. He was struck by the fact that the responses he observed in infants to child-care practices were in line with broad expectations for behavior in both cultures. For example, in the United States the expectation that the individual should be physically and verbally assertive, and in Japan, that the individual should be physically and verbally restrained, was observable in infant behavior as well as in child rearing. During my fieldwork in East Africa in the mid-1970s, I was similarly struck with how cultural values interacted with the constitutional characteristics of the baby.

From the cross-cultural perspective, two points emerge that are of interest regarding this volume. One is that the culture and the family project their ideas as to what an infant can actually do, often with very good evolutionary and social reasons, and thereby shape the infant's behavior. The other is that infants are capable of an immense repertoire of behavior at birth and during the first year, a fact borne out over 40 years of ethnographic and experimental study. These two aspects, that the infant is receptive to learning and can carry out an immense range of behavior, as well as being open to shaping by family and culture, provide the rationale for this book.

Ms. Boucke provides a practical update and guide to potty training, using observations of infants and maternal comments. In so doing she follows in the footsteps of earlier anthropological field studies dating to Geber. These cross-cultural studies have illuminated the diverse perspectives and the range of possibilities available to Western mothers. In photos, testimonials and descriptive material, Ms. Boucke brings this information to the Western reader in practical down-home language. The lesson from Ms. Boucke and traditional societies is that infant potty training is far more than just a chore or messy necessity, it is an important way for the family and baby to get to know one another. Boucke refutes the Western views that early training is coercive or potentially dangerous in terms of personality formation, using a world sample to show that potty training can indeed be a nurturant experience and help create a competent infant. Her selection of photos and comments make it clear that potty training can be anything but harsh.

Today, given the advance of diaper technology, it is not necessary for families to employ the time-tested method of infant toilet training. But this is a valid and effective alternative, as Ms. Boucke makes clear with examples from Asia, Africa and the USA. Her books *Infant Potty Training* and *Infant Potty Basics* provide the opportunity for mothers to be with their infants in new, creative and loving ways. I find that the author's practical advice and clear descriptions constitute a nurturant contribution to families, pediatricians and child-rearing literature in general.

Marten W. deVries
Maastricht, 2000

Chapter 1
Some Basic Questions

This book is about communicating and working with infants towards lovingly, gently and gradually accomplishing what is commonly known as "potty training," "toilet learning," and so on. But don't confuse this method with mainstream Western toilet training. The ideal time to start infant pottying is sometime between birth and 4–5 months of age, when the first window of opportunity is open for this type of learning.

Perhaps the most unique characteristic of this method is that parents typically begin working with a baby before she can even sit on her own. Instead of beginning research on toilet training around the time a child takes her first steps, the best time for parents to consider this method is during pregnancy or the first weeks/months after delivery.

Who Can Use This Method?

This book is intended for parents of infants, parents-to-be, grandparents, nannies and anyone else interested in lovingly and patiently working with an infant towards toilet independence at the earliest possible age. "Infant" is the operative word here, as opposed to "toddler," in that a caregiver begins working as a team with an infant in the early months of life.

This method does not claim to be *the* method for everybody, but parents should at least know the facts about it when considering how to toilet train their children. Pediatricians and other members of the medical community should be knowledgeable enough to discuss this method with inquisitive parents. Infant pottying is best used by:

- a parent who spends at least the first 1–2 years caring for baby
- a working parent with a trustworthy and reliable helper (family member, nanny or friend) or team of helpers readily available

What Does It Take?

Time, diligence, patience and practice. If you cannot devote these qualities or arrange for any assistance you may need, this is not the method for you or your baby.

How Long Does It Take?

Infant potty learning is a gradual developmental and communication process that carries on for many months, not unlike learning to walk or talk. As with other major skills, it takes months of practice. Parents who start sometime before their baby is 5 months old should expect to finish around the age of 2 years. Many finish around 18 months, but in order to have a relaxed and patient mindset, parents should be prepared to spend the maximum number of months. If you finish earlier, it will be a bonus. The youngest age of completion that I have experienced in the USA is 10 months (See Chapter 10 for more), but this is highly unusual and should not be your goal. Consider this method as something akin to breastfeeding in terms of time, intimacy and bonding. It takes a dedicated and loving caregiver. This is not a method for parents in a hurry. Expecting too much too soon can lead to giving up.

Mothers who don't limit themselves to the standard Western definition of "toilet trained" are more open to recognizing, appreciating and enjoying different degrees and stages of evolution along the way—and this new outlook yields a different answer to the question of how long it takes. Depending on circumstances (age started; individual learning curve; good health; positive environment; consistency of caregiver(s); etc.) and one's definition of the term "potty trained" (ability to re-lease on cue; ability to retain and wait to go; importance or lack of clothing factors; total potty independence), it generally takes from 6 months to 2 years.

Is It Safe?

Of course! Every effort has been made to provide proper and safe guidelines for holding and working with your baby. If the guidelines are followed correctly, no psychological or physical harm can occur to your baby. Punishment, anger and control are *not* a part of this method. Instead, parents must exercise patience and gentleness; observe and respond to baby's signals on time whenever reasonably possible; and use intelligent, caring and loving caution when handling their infants.

How Do I Know When My Baby Needs to Go?

You can know when baby needs to go by one or more of the following:

- timing (by the clock)
- signals and cues (including body language and sound)
- patterns in elimination timing
- intuition and instinct

Does It Really Work?

Yes, but not without practice and effort. Success does not just happen on its own. It takes at least one committed adult and several months of perseverance to complete infant potty training. In most situations, there are daily rewards for both baby and caregiver right from the very first days or weeks. Baby's communication is acknowledged and encouraged. Parents are amazed at the degree of their infant's awareness and are thrilled when experiencing this special form of communication and responsiveness with their infant.

Does My Baby Have to Be Naked?

This is not a requirement. Many parents keep a diaper or training pants on their baby in between potty visits, while others prefer to leave their baby bare-bottomed or naked most of the time. In short, it is a matter of preference and a lifestyle choice.

Can I Still Start If My Baby Is 6 Months or Older?

If this method resonates, if it sounds right for you and your baby, yes, it is fine to give it a try (despite all the scare tactics to the contrary). Although the first and most effective window of learning generally ends around age 4–5 months, some babies remain receptive beyond this. And other windows of opportunity open at different times during a child's development. For example, many babies are again ready for toilet learning around the age of 8–12 months, 18 months and/or 24 months. Since each child is unique, there is no way to know for sure when yours will again be receptive to toilet learning once she is older than 5 months. Depending on the age of your baby, you may have to slightly modify some approaches.

Can I Do It Part Time or with Daycare?

Many families do. If you are fairly consistent, it is not confusing for your child. Strive to potty your baby on a fairly regular basis during optimal and obvious times when you are at home, such as first thing in the morning, after naps, before bed, at night (if you decide to get up), on weekends and holidays. Elicit the help of other family members including siblings. Some families train a trusted caregiver who stays at home with their baby during the work hours. Others combine IPT with home-schooling older siblings. If you plan to send your baby to daycare, search for one that is open to IPT or that is willing to potty your baby every so often, perhaps along with the toddlers. At the very least, they should be willing to change your baby often.

Does It Work with a Toddler and a Baby or with Twins?

Many families first hear about IPT when they have a toddler and a baby. It is fine to use IPT with both. The same applies to families with twins. On the one hand, your time will be limited compared to a family with just one child, but on the other hand, two or more children tend to encourage, inspire and motivate each other with regard to toilet learning. By using part-time IPT, you will keep the children's elimination awareness alive and thus enable them to control elimination at the earliest moment possible for them.

Will People Think I'm Crazy?

There are people who object to every lifestyle imaginable, so don't let this deter you. Since the 1950s, the Western world has been indoctrinated to fear and reject any form of early toilet learning. In fact, infant elimination training has been suppressed and eradicated from our national psyche, so in this sense, we face an uphill battle. Even when our own parents or grandparents tell us that they had all of their children potty trained by 8–12 months, we tend to disbelieve them and assume they are exaggerating.

Happily, the tide is turning and word is spreading. Many new and expecting parents are open and objective enough to weigh the pros and cons of this method. They are extremely excited when they hear about it and do not appreciate the fact that they have been kept in the dark for so long. There are now pediatricians and other medical professionals who support the infant potty technique. More and more Westerners are beginning to recognize the fact that there is a lot of money, rather than truth and sound research, behind some big product endorsements (diapers and bestselling books come to mind) and are less frightened by the lobbying against infant elimination training. As awareness spreads, there will be less resistance to, and consternation about, this gentle method.

What Are the Main Benefits?

The three big winners are baby, parent(s) and the environment. Here is a more complete list:

- Enhances bonding through closeness, natural communication and loving patience.
- Responds to infants' natural elimination communication and timing.
- Taps into first window of learning (sensitivity period) for toilet learning.
- Keeps babies in touch with their own bodies.
- Helps environment by conserving/saving trees, water, petroleum and landfill space.
- Cuts diaper use.
- Allows babies to achieve good control by 12–15 months.
- Lets babies complete potty training at a relatively young age (around 24 months).
- Frees babies from diapers and all negative associations (bulk between legs, chemicals, etc.).
- Reduces risk of urinary tract infections (UTIs).
- Avoids/eliminates enuresis (bed wetting).
- Prevents diaper rash.
- Provides hygienic respect for babies by freeing them from their waste.
- Eliminates embarrassing "accidents" for toddlers.
- Allows fathers or other close, trusted ones to bond and communicate with babies.
- Yields big savings on diapers and laundry costs.

Isn't It Really the Mother Who Is Trained?

At first, it is mainly up to mothers to get things started. But after a few hours, days or weeks, babies become very active participants. Just as we gladly help our babies with many other things such as eating, dressing and bathing, many find it enjoyable and hygienic to help their babies eliminate into receptacles rather than into diapers or pants. All these activities at first take training on the part of mothers. And just as we encourage and help our babies master other important skills such as walking or talking over many months, we can help them with toileting by giving them the chance to repeatedly practice pottying, and by positively and gently reinforcing what they learn. In short, infant pottying involves mother-baby teamwork. It starts out with some "mother training" but soon progresses to "baby-mother training" since baby-mother interaction and communication are the keys.

Can Fathers Help with IPT?

Certainly! The more support and help from fathers, the better. If a father is hesitant about toileting his own baby, the next best thing is to provide positive feedback to mother and child, and to take on household tasks whenever possible, in order to "free up" mom so she can concentrate on IPT. But most fathers are delighted to take a more active role. If you want to participate, take your child to "go" in the morning before work, in the afternoon and evening after work, on weekends and holidays and, if your family elects to get up for IPT at night, during the night. Fathers who are interested have the ability to be in tune with their babies, to become familiar with elimination timing and patterns, to recognize their babies' elimination signals and to intuitively know when their babies need to go.

What Is the Author's Experience with Toilet Teaching?

When my first child was born, I knew almost nothing about babies. And so, as happens with many new mothers, I was trained to train my first son to use diapers. I dutifully followed suit with my second son. Both experienced conventional Western toilet training. When my third son was born, I dreaded the thought of additional years of diapers and began seeking a better solution.

I learned the basis for an alternative technique through a lady visiting us from India. She was horrified when I told her the way Westerners handle the "waste disposal issue" and explained to me the way things are done "back home" in her culture. I was skeptical when she told me that there is no need to use "the cloths" on an infant unless it is "ill of the stomach," feverish or wets the bed most nights. I had been to India several times and had noticed families peeing and pooing their babies around the countryside, but had not paid close attention. Like many others, I mistakenly assumed that Westerners could not use this technique.

I begged my new friend to tell me more and to teach me how to hold my son and get him to go for me, which she gladly and effortlessly did. I was spellbound watching her communicate with my tiny 3-month-old son, who somehow instinctively knew what she wanted him to do. I can only describe the exchange and instant understanding between them—a stranger and an infant—as a wonderful discovery.

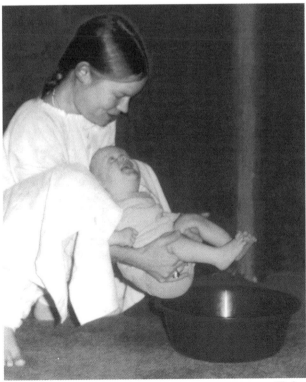

Khalsa

The author demonstrates the in-arms position with her son.

I used the technique she demonstrated, slightly modifying and adapting it to a Western lifestyle, and found it to be far superior to conventional diaper-to-potty-training. From the day I started working with my 3-month-old son, he rarely needed a diaper, day or night. He stayed dry during most of the day at age 18 months and was finished at 25 months. But more important than "finishing early" were the closeness, bonding and communication we shared.

Is There Some Terminology To Help Me?

There is no English term to suitably describe infant pottying as a whole, since (a) an infant cannot sit alone on a potty or toilet and (b) the process is more about communication, responsiveness and interconnectedness than about actual toilet training. The toilet learning is a by-product of following your basic maternal instincts.

Different expressions are used to describe this method, and you will encounter these as you read articles or books and travel around the Internet. Some of the names in use are:

- elimination communication (EC) and elimination timing (ET)
- infant potty training, infant potty technique, infant potty teamwork, infant potty teaching and intuitive potty training (IPT)
- diaperless, diaper free and natural infant hygiene (NIH)
- trickle treat (TT)

In this book, lay terminology is used with a view to reaching the average reader and family. Thus, the word "go" is frequently used to mean "eliminate." The term "pee" is used to mean "urinate," and the terms "poo" and "poop" are used to mean "defecate" and "defecation." The words "potty" and "toilet" are sometimes used as verbs in the generic sense of "pottying or toileting baby" and when used this way do not necessarily refer to any specific receptacles for elimination.

In the expression "infant potty training," the word "training" is used in the positive sense of a loving exchange between mother and baby. It refers to a form of mother-baby training and synergy, and should *never* be misconstrued in the negative sense of pressure, rigidity or coercion.

Instead of awkwardly referring to baby as "s/he," "he or she" and "his/her," this book uses one single gender throughout a particular chapter unless there are obvious references where the opposite sex applies. Hence, Chapter 3 generically refers to baby in the feminine gender (she, her, hers), whereas Chapter 4 generically refers to baby in the masculine gender (he, him, his).

Finally, ages in months and years are given in digits (2 months old) rather than words (two months old). This makes it easier to scan through the text and find a reference to a particular age. This applies everywhere except in quoted material where authors' original styles are preserved.

Chapter 2
Philosophy and Attitude

Babies are smarter and more receptive than we think. The big mistake we make is to presume that a newborn baby is unaware of going to the toilet. We assume an infant is incapable of toilet learning since he is small and uncoordinated and because he cannot walk or talk. An infant is helpless in so many ways that it is hard for Westerners to imagine such a tiny being could be aware of peeing and pooing. It is even harder for us to believe that an infant has some control over his elimination. With these preconceived and narrow views, we encourage and teach our babies to be unconcerned about wetting and soiling diapers. In short, we teach our infants to use diapers as a toilet.

A normal, healthy infant is indeed aware of the bodily function of elimination and can learn to respond to it from infancy. By using diapers, we condition and thereby train baby to go in them. Later the child must unlearn this training. This can be confusing and a traumatic experience for the child. But conditioning can work in a positive sense too. Studies of conditioning in babies demonstrate that newborns are able to learn and remember things, so it is up to you to gently and lovingly guide and encourage your infant. It is important to note that infant pottying cannot work if you use punishment, coercion, pressure and/or anger. It takes a positive attitude and a relaxed mama (or other caregiver).

If you do not believe that an infant is aware of elimination, take his diaper off and observe him as he pees or poos. From his facial expressions to his body language and vocalizations, you will see and hear that he is aware of what is going on. He is in touch with these muscles and sensations, and it is your job to help keep him in touch and to encourage further muscular development. Like any other muscle, the more a baby consciously experiences and begins to exercise his sphincter muscles, the more control he can gain. At first it may just be a sensation on his part, but he will inevitably experiment with contracting and relaxing the muscles. The earlier you acknowledge this and encourage him to continue, the earlier he can gain some control. When you work with this control, instead of against it by ignoring or denying it, toilet learning can usually be completed much sooner than expected in the West.

An infant does his best to communicate his awareness to you, but if you don't watch and listen, he will stop communicating and gradually lose touch with the elimination functions. He will be conditioned not to care and will learn that you want him to use his diaper as a toilet.

Babies are creatures of habit and instinct. The younger you teach them something they are ready to learn, the easier it is for them to learn it. Infants send signals and are very receptive to your communication about their elimination, unless this awareness is suppressed by the constant use of diapers.

One of the first mistakes is letting a baby become comfortable with his wet- · ness. If he is allowed to wear his toilet by experiencing a wet diaper on a regular basis, he will grow accustomed to feeling wet and lose his natural aversion to this sensation. This will make toilet teaching a more difficult task, no matter when you begin. If you use super-absorbent disposable diapers that always make baby feel dry by absorbing the urine into a gel, he will not learn to associate urination with wetness. When he finally begins toilet learning in earnest, whether at age 15 months or 4 years, it is likely to be difficult for him to make the cause-and-effect connection between peeing and feeling wet.

If you use diapers, remove his diaper as soon as he wets, to avoid his becoming accustomed to wetness. Whenever possible, use cloth diapers without a waterproof cover in order to immediately feel any dampness and remove the wet diaper. Let him remain bare-bottomed at intervals throughout the day. He will be more comfortable without a constant bulk between his legs.

Diapers, especially disposable ones, are a convenient but temporary solution to the toilet situation. We attempt to "plug up" our child's disposal system with diapers in the same way as we temporarily stop the flow from a leaking pipe. How many parents have pondered whether or not this is a hygienic solution for the child? How many parents care about the effects of diapers on the environment? How many would care if they knew of an alternative to full-time diapers?

Another way to look at an infant's natural ability to respond to elimination communication is to compare it to a Montessori "sensitive period" in that the optimum learning time for many things is in infancy when the brain is open and receptive. A sensitive period refers to a time during infancy when a child can learn certain things through natural absorption. If the child misses the timing of this learning, he will later have to work or struggle at learning it. An infant can learn potty techniques effortlessly and with joy, just as children can learn foreign languages with no effort and no accent at a young age, something that later becomes an arduous process.

Babies in non-Western societies typically complete toilet learning far earlier than Western babies. In some respects, Western mothers using infant pottying face an uphill battle. The very concept strikes many as ridiculous, impracticable or impossible, so a mother opting for this method does not have the societal support and examples that teach, inspire and sustain mothers in traditional societies. Most women abroad have experienced infant elimination training themselves. It is and has long been the norm for them, so that women and children have a life experience of loving support from both their families and communities. Due to many generations of unwavering acceptance and positive acculturation in their societies, the attitude towards infant toilet learning is nurturing and tranquil. No one finds it unusual or strange. No doctors or psychologists frighten families with stories of psychological damage caused by infant pottying. In these cultures, babies generally don't wear diapers and are not subjected to anger, impatience, punishment or worries about keeping carpeting or fancy clothing clean and dry. They do not have to undergo diaper untraining and are free to run and play as toddlers, without interruption by boring and confining diaper changes and potty sessions.

Not only is toilet teaching from infancy basically unheard of in Western countries, it also strikes many as inconvenient. With relatively few exceptions, however, toilet training is by definition inconvenient no matter when you begin.

Infant pottying can be approached in a rational and scientific manner as well as an intuitive and spiritual one—or a combination of both—depending on what works best for you and your baby. The rational approach involves timing and observation of elimination patterns and baby body language. The more spiritual approach involves intuition and tuning in to your baby in more subtle ways. Both are covered in detail. Remember: *It is teamwork, something you do together. It is not something you are doing to your baby, and it is not something your baby can do without you.*

Infant potty teamwork creates a special feeling of intimacy and closeness between parent and baby. Your infant will enjoy being held in your arms, touching your face, patting your hands and caressing you. You will enjoy cuddling him in your arms as you gaze at each other, directly or via a mirror. All of this enhances bonding and communication.

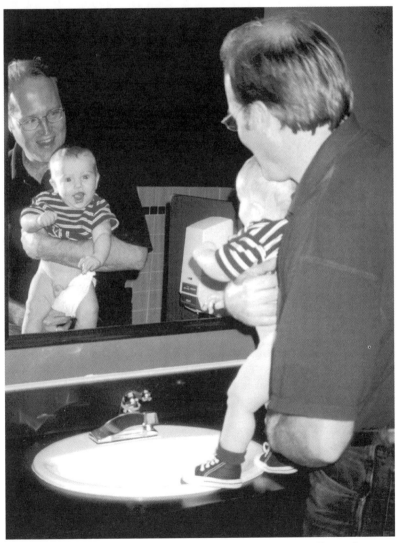

Vanessa Lorentzen

4 months old — Looking in the mirror is great fun.
Zion's favorite position is "in-arms standing" rather than squatting.

A positive, confident and consistent attitude on the part of parents and all others involved cannot be overemphasized. Without the right attitude on your part, you cannot expect to reap all the benefits. It is important to make toilet time a relaxing and enjoyable time for your baby. This can only be accomplished if you practice patience and exude encouragement and confidence.

Together you accomplish an amazing feat. Express your joy and satisfaction in whatever way feels most natural and spontaneous to you. Some mothers display their excitement by clapping, praising or otherwise celebrating, while others prefer to be matter-of-fact and simply remark, "You peed," or, "You pooed," without showing much emotion.

At first you may need to discipline yourself to be available on time for baby whenever reasonably possible. Do not punish him (or yourself!) if you arrive too late. Avoid making him feel like a failure if he wets his pants and/or goes in the wrong place. If he accidentally goes on the floor, furniture, bedspread, etc., don't despair and don't blame him. Just clean up and move on. When he wobbles, stumbles and falls while practicing walking, you will not feel angry or frustrated but will encourage his attempts. The same attitude applies to pottying—it is normal to experience many spills over the months, just as you expect your baby to take many falls while he is learning to walk.

Be open-minded. If your child wets his clothing, try to determine why. It may be due to illness, travel, emotional problems, a change in schedule or a change in baby's natural body rhythms. If the schedule or rhythms have changed, as they will do a number of times over the months as he grows and matures, be alert and flexible enough to change with your child. Mothers who nurse on demand and rely mainly on timing to know when baby needs to pee may at first find it tricky to anticipate when he needs to go. Since he nurses whenever he pleases rather than at fixed intervals, he is likely to pee and poo at irregular intervals. In this situation, strive to learn your baby's body language, vocalizations and other signals. Observe when he evacuates in relation to breastfeeding bouts. Trust and make use of your intuition.

It is also up to you to provide a cozy and peaceful environment. Your baby must never feel under pressure to perform. This means that you cannot be in a rush. If you find you do not have the time to correctly and peacefully potty him on some occasions, do not hesitate to use a diaper at those times. It is far better to do so than to project negative feelings onto your baby. If you're feeling exhausted, take a break and go back to training pants or diapers. It's better to have a pee or a poo in the pants than to get stressed out.

Every one of us occasionally experiences a "bad day." If you are tense or in a bad mood, gain control over your negative emotions so you do not direct them at your child. Babies can instantly sense when you are upset and negative. They detect your mood in things like your behavior, facial expressions, tone of voice, body movements, muscular tension and breathing. Teach yourself to accept the fact that you will make mistakes. If you "miss" several pees or poos and find that baby's elimination is "out of sink" (sync), don't become distraught and don't assign blame. *IPT is not an all-or-nothing endeavor.* It is unrealistic to expect perfection from yourself or your baby until the process is complete. Consider yourselves to be gradually working towards eventual perfection, knowing it will take many months, mishaps, cuddles and laughs to reach that goal. The difference between a good day and a bad day is often not so much the things that happen but your attitude towards them, whether you can relax and laugh about them or not.

Babies also have the occasional "off day." On such occasions, they may not give their usual signal(s), or you might miss their signals. If a baby is ill or if there is a change in his daily routine, this can throw his timing off for a while. No blame or guilt should be assigned. Pay closer attention to your baby and resynchronize with him as soon as possible. This could take a number of days in some situations.

Find a balance between the following:

- The more regularly and faithfully you adhere to IPT, the more likely your child will be diaper free at the earliest moment possible.
- It is better to occasionally resort to diapers (and this is not a failure on your part if you do so) than to wear yourself out or direct anger and frustration at your child.

In other words, be as consistent as possible but not to the point of becoming stressed, obsessed, exhausted or frustrated. Sometimes we try too hard and make too big a deal out of toileting. Remember, a relaxed flow is essential. You can't expect to be there for every pee, just as you can't expect to be there for every baby step or every time your baby mispronounces a word.

When your child is old enough to use a potty, he should never be forced to sit on it for long periods of time. A good range is 2–10 minutes, depending on the age and attention span of the child. This does not mean you should let your child avoid potty time altogether. Be firm in your convictions by finding creative ways to encourage him to sit on the pot. When necessary, entertain, distract or fascinate baby to keep him on the potty. Take a break if he doesn't go at the expected time, then come back a while later to try again. Do not use force or other negative emotions. Potty time should be pleasant.

This method is not about control. If you frequently get into a battle of wills, you might as well resort to conventional potty training methods. Strive to remain neutral, nonchalant and nonjudgmental while at the same time letting baby know potty time is a necessary and serious part of life.

A frequently asked question is: "If I'm not consistent on a regular basis, will this confuse my baby?" As long as you are fairly regular for some potty sessions each day, you will not confuse your child. Many mothers keep their babies apprised of the situation, "I can't get you to the potty while we're out driving around (or homeschooling or working in the office—fill in the blank) so you need to use diapers in the afternoon."

What *is* confusing is to be erratic and irregular, only taking baby to pee when it is convenient for you. Those convenient times will dwindle until they disappear altogether. In addition, once baby senses that you aren't really serious about communicating and working together, he may stop signaling you.

Contrary to what many doctors may tell you, there is not one method of toilet teaching that is ideal for every parent, child, home situation and lifestyle. You may find yourself in a position to use this method with one child and not with your next, depending on your domestic situation or your frame of mind.

The main drawback to infant toilet learning is that it is time consuming, but all methods take time in one form or another. Infancy is a logical time to start since a small child requires a lot of time and attention anyway. By responding to baby's natural timing and signals, you reinforce his instinctive awareness of and communication about elimination. Both of you will benefit greatly from the time you devote to this technique. If you are willing and able, your baby is ready for you.

Chapter 3
The In-Arms Phase

The two main phases of infant potty teamwork are the:

- in-arms phase (anytime from birth, for as long as baby needs considerable physical support at potty time)
- potty/toilet-seat phase (begins when baby can sit comfortably and independently on a potty or toilet)

The in-arms phase is the most crucial and, for Westerners, unique part of infant pottying. Since an infant cannot sit independently, she should be cradled securely and comfortably in your arms over a receptacle or other toilet place for this phase.

The optimum time to begin this phase is anytime from birth through 3 to 4 months of age since this is the first window of opportunity. Starting at birth or before the 4th or 5th month generally yields faster and better results than starting at the age of 6 months or older. If you begin after 6 months, you will most likely need to modify some of the techniques. In short, there is no definite cutoff point, but typically, the earlier you start, the better.

Infant pottying is much more intense and demanding at the start (partly because babies pee more often in infancy and also because you are adjusting to many other aspects of infancy), gradually becomes easier and less time consuming over the months and is often completed sooner than traditional methods (although this is not the primary goal). In the long run, it takes no more time than full-time diapering methods and in some cases takes (considerably) less time. But it's not about breaking any records or doing better than your neighbor or sister. It's about you and your infant communicating and bonding through mutual adoration and intrinsic involvement with each other.

The six steps of the in-arms phase are:

1. Choosing Your Basic Signal
2. Timing and Elimination Patterns
3. Selecting a Location and/or Receptacle
4. Positions
5. Signals and Cues
6. Understanding and Commitment

STEP 1: Choosing Your Basic Signal

The first step involves selecting a signal to cue baby to go for you. Your signal can be any sound you choose. The most common signal for voiding is to imitate the sound of running water or urination, "sssss" or "pssss." For defecation, you can use a grunting or straining sound such as "hmmmm," or just use "sssss" for both forms of elimination. Some parents prefer baby talk such as "pee pee" while others like to use a sentence with recognizable voice intonation, "Do you have to pee?" Some mothers rely on the position to be the "cue de grace" and do not use any audible signal. Use whatever feels most natural and comfortable to you. Infants can learn to associate their elimination with your cues in just a few days if you start early enough.

STEP 2: Timing and Elimination Patterns

Step 2 involves familiarization with baby's natural timing and elimination patterns. You can gain a general feeling for baby's elimination timing during one or more sessions of about 30 minutes to an hour or two, whatever feels right for you.

Select a warm, comfortable, well-lighted place for observing the child. Lay some protective material on the carpet or mattress. Suggestions include a layer of waterproof material covered with a sheet and either a few towels or a cloth diaper. If the fountain effect proves to be a problem with a baby boy during this exercise, you can put a diaper, flannel blanket or soft towel over his groin area. Bear in mind that if you cover his penis, you may have to pay closer attention to ascertain exactly when he pees.

If you find it helpful to make notations (not everyone does), you will need a pen, watch and writing paper. Make a note of when you feed your baby. It's easier, but not essential, to start with a feeding which is not directly followed by a nap. Jot down the times you start and finish the feeding.

When baby pees or poos during and/or after the feeding, make the "sssss" sound and jot down the time. Making the "sssss" sound helps baby learn to associate your basic signal with elimination. If she makes a sound or you notice a physical body signal just before she eliminates, use this to help you anticipate future elimination. Remove the wet cloth and replace it with a clean, dry one. Repeat the process for as many times as baby pees after the feeding. The object of the exercise is to eventually use your notes to determine the frequency of your baby's need to urinate and any patterns in relation to feeding and sleeping.

If you're observing a newborn and still recovering from delivery, or if you don't want to leave your baby (partially) unclothed for observation, another way to study your baby's elimination timing is to place a diaper on your chest, lay baby on the diaper, wait for her to go, give your basic signal when she pees or poos and jot down the time of elimination. Replace the wet or soiled cloth with a clean, dry one, and repeat this process as many times as necessary.

You can also study timing and patterns while using a sling. Baby-wearing is one of the best ways to become familiar and stay in tune with your baby's elimination timing and patterns since you know straightaway when she goes. It is especially beneficial in cold climates or rooms without sufficient heating. Some mothers keep their babies naked in the sling, carrying them skin-to-skin, which keeps baby at a perfect body temperature. If so desired, you can keep a cloth diaper under her while in the sling. It is, of course, not a requirement to keep your baby naked in the sling. Even if she is wearing some clothing and/or a cloth diaper without a waterproof cover, you will know when she goes.

Mothers who use their intuition to know when baby needs to go may only need to rely on timing to get started. Some may even skip this step altogether and instead rely exclusively on the intuitive connection with their babies. Trust your instincts and abilities. If you feel, have a hunch or simply *know* it is time for baby to pee, offer her a chance to go for you. Most mothers sense other things by instinct and intuition, such as when their baby is tired, hungry or ill. In a way similar to automatically knowing when to respond to these things for baby, you can help her relieve herself at the right moment too.

As you observe your baby, you will likely begin to note that there are "toilet patterns" in relation to when she eats and sleeps. Many babies urinate at fairly regular intervals, depending on the time of eating and sleeping. For example, newborns and small infants might pee once every 5–15 minutes for a number of times after a feeding. As babies grow older, they go less frequently. A 3-month-old might pee every 15–20 minutes three or four times after nursing, and then the interval between pees might increase to 30 minutes, or else baby might just pee once after 30 minutes and then not need to go again until she eats again. Other toilet patterns to expect are peeing or pooing upon waking and also during or soon after a feeding—although some babies don't need to go for 10–15 minutes after nursing.

Always remember that the timing used in IPT is based on baby's timing and patterns, rather than on your own. If you potty her every 15–20 minutes after feedings, it is because you have learned this from her. Even if you feel that potty visits are hit-or-miss based on an educated guess, your guess should be based on your observations and feelings about when your baby needs to go. And other factors can come into play here. For example, if baby is tired, ill or cold, she may pee more often. If in a warm climate or if dressed warmly, she may pee less frequently than usual.

Bear in mind that baby's timing and patterns will change from time to time as she grows and as her bladder capacity increases. Every so often, try waiting a little longer between toilet visits—maybe stretch it from going every 20 minutes to going every 30 minutes. If she does okay, use the new timing. If she isn't ready, go back to the earlier pattern for a while longer.

If your baby tends to go while breastfeeding, seat her on a receptacle, such as a small bowl or small potty, while nursing her. Find a position that is comfortable. The key to learning baby's timing is to relate elimination to feeding and waking. An attentive mother will instinctively sense or eventually recognize a correlation between these components.

Finally, there are exceptions to every rule. Not all babies have a regular or predictable elimination pattern, so don't be alarmed or discouraged if you can't find a pattern. It can be a challenge for beginners to catch an elusive and enigmatic pee or poo. The first catches may seem like pure chance. Some mothers start out by relying on the clock. Using a timer can be helpful for this until timing becomes second nature. Others do really well the first day or week, then seem to lose the knack for a while. Some mothers have an easy time with pees but not poos, while others do well with poos but can't seem to get their baby to pee for them for days or even weeks. Some babies have very irregular or infrequent bowel movements (breastfed babies might only poo once every 7–10 days), which can make it difficult or impossible to "score" for a while. You may have to rely more on signals, cues, body language, intuition and/or a combination of (some of) these to first get in sync with your baby. And later you may find yourself using some or all of them to different degrees as your baby changes over time.

STEP 3: Selecting a Location and/or Receptacle

Before proceeding any further, you will have to select a "toilet place" and receptacle. For the first few days or weeks, it is advisable to use the same place and receptacle(s) whenever possible so baby associates these with the functions of elimination. Using different receptacles for urine and bowel movements is acceptable (but not mandatory) for reasons of hygiene and also because the receptacle used to catch a bowel movement may be less accessible or less convenient to use.

A myriad of receptacles and locations are functional, and here you can bring your creativity into play. Select whatever container and location suit you, your child and your situation best. One of the most popular places for urination is the bathroom sink. For peeing, you can also use the shower. Receptacles for both urination and bowel movements include a potty, small baking/mixing bowl, plastic rectangular basin, toilet, bidet, pet bowl, food container, bucket (ideally with a tight-fitting lid) or any other catchall that works. If you seat your baby on a vessel, it should be "baby-bottom friendly" in terms of size, comfort and temperature. If you live or camp in the wilderness, mother nature offers many an interesting toilet place for infants.

Gunnar Dibbern
5-month-old Janus taking a relaxing pee at the beach
in Germany after a day out and about.

If you use the bathroom sink, most babies enjoy the mirror, but like everything else, this is subjective. In some cases it may prove to be (or eventually become) too distracting for a baby to watch her reflection. With every phase of infant potty teamwork, parents find that certain approaches work well for a while, then need to change as their babies change and grow. And certain approaches work with some children but not with others. *There is not a fixed way to "do" infant pottying.* Everyone progresses it in the way that works best for their own family.

STEP 4: Positions

The classic "elimination position" resembles sitting in a chair or squatting in-arms. For neonates, let baby lie flat on her back in your arms, with her head touching your chest or abdomen (depending on the height of your sink or receptacle). For both of these positions, hold baby's thighs in your hands, spreading the thighs slightly apart while "aiming" her over the sink or other toilet place. Take care not to pull her knees up too high and also not to squish or otherwise apply pressure to her belly. As baby grows, you'll need more arm space to accommodate her height, and you can cradle her in your arms by resting her back between your forearms and leaning her head against your chest. Most babies find this position relaxing. Many variations are possible. For newborns, it may be more comfortable to rest baby on one arm while grasping her feet with the same arm, and supporting her head with the other hand.

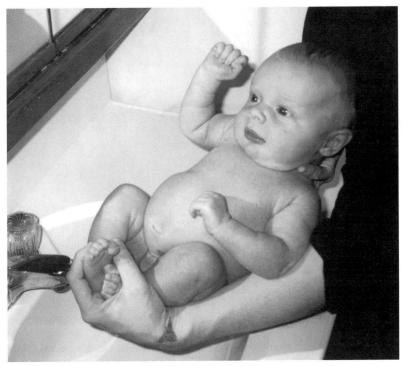

Matt Jasper

3-week-old Albion admires himself in the mirror.
His mother discovered it was a good idea to hold his feet together because:
(a) holding him under each thigh was making his legs turn purple and
(b) it was easier to hold his legs up and aim his stream downward.

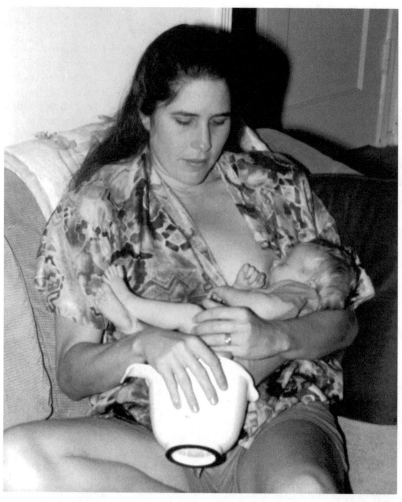

Tom Griggs

2 weeks old — Holding a small baking bowl under Sara's bottom
allows her to nurse uninterrupted while her mother becomes
familiar with her timing and elimination patterns.

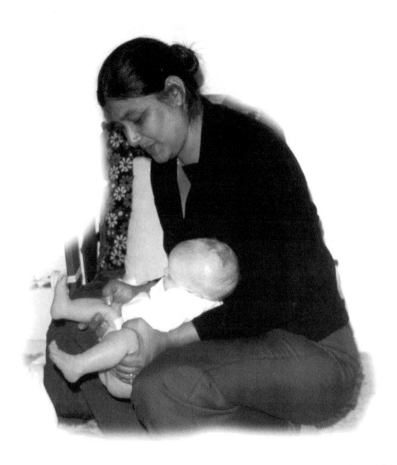

Laurie Boucke

3 months old — Classic squatting position for both mother and baby.
Caregiver squats. Baby's head and neck are supported by caregiver's
chest and arm, baby's back rests against adult's knees. Baby is held
in position by the thighs. In Western countries, it is more common for
the mother to stand at the sink, holding baby in the same position.

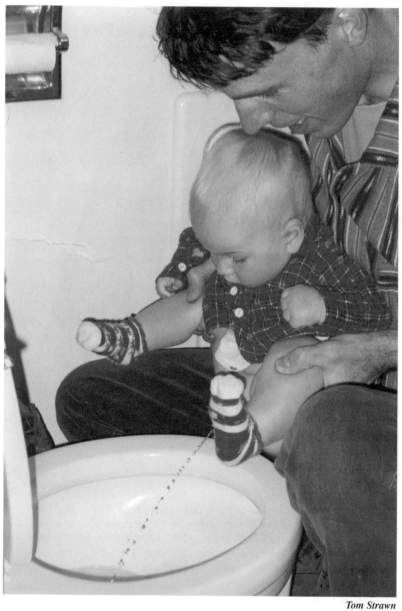

Tom Strawn

5-month-old Aidan is right on target.

Craig Baas

Zachary at 7 months, with mother Lois.

Brett Cornish Scott

7-month-old Aedhan watches his stream with great interest
before waving bye-bye to the puddle on the ground.

Gunnar Dibbern

6-month-old Janus pees from a park bench
in 36°F weather in Germany. His mother Julia says,
"He always pees when we stop at this park bench."

Kevin White

2-month-old McKenna goes in the yard as her
Poquito Pants remain dry on the porch railing.

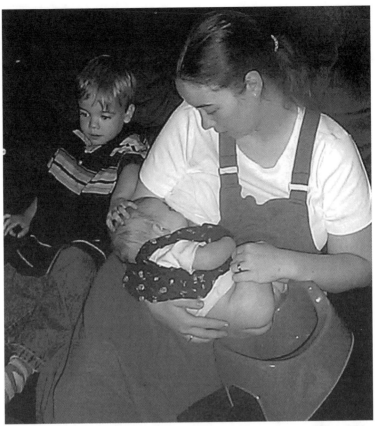

Kevin White

2-month-old McKenna nurses over the potty
as her brother gives some TLC.

Whatever position you use, it is your responsibility to provide the following:

- comfortable, secure and relaxing position
- proper support for the neck, head and spine
- warm, hygienic and peaceful surroundings
- positive attitude

With boys, more attention is needed for aiming since urination lifts the penis. One means is to use a fingertip to aim him downward when the stream starts to rise. Another is to aim baby's body as best you can, then cup your hand to direct the stream, in effect using your palm as a splashguard. With a toilet or bucket, hang baby's bottom deep enough so that the stream remains in the receptacle. Small boys, and even some girls, generally enjoy watching their stream, and this reinforces awareness. When old enough to sit well on a toilet, boys can straddle the seat further back and shoot into the bowl without assistance.

Lois Baas (from video)

11-month-old Zachary taking care of business.

Caregivers with physical limitations can seek alternative ways to hold or support baby. If you experience back pain or if a young sibling finds baby heavy to hold in position, one solution is to hold baby in your lap while you sit on the toilet, serving as a warm human cushion and taking the weight off your back. A variation is to sit on the toilet and hold baby between your legs. For this position, you can hold baby in either a squatting or sitting position, with her back against your abdomen or thighs. You can face either way on the toilet; some babies like to face the back of the toilet while others prefer facing forward.

If you find that the positions described in this chapter are not right for you and your baby, gently experiment until you find one that works well for both of you. Bear in mind that a favorite position can one day be unexpectedly rejected by your baby, in which case you'll need to find an alternative. And some babies are comfy and happy in a number of different positions.

STEP 5: Signals and Cues

The next step is for caregiver and baby to develop the ability to read and respond to each other's cues. This can be done on various levels and differs from child to child and parent to parent.

Signals from Caregiver to Baby . . .

Before signaling, bear in mind that baby will only respond to your signals if she has to go. If her bladder is full or nearly full, or if she needs to poo soon, she has the ability to *release* the contents upon receiving your cue(s). If she does not need to go, she will not respond to your cues, and you should not insist. There are exceptions in that some infants will listen to your cue, then grunt, bear down, thrust their pelvis or concentrate and release a small amount of urine even if their bladder is not very full.

For many babies, the most predictable times to eliminate are upon waking first thing in the morning, upon waking up from a long nap, while nursing or a certain amount of time after nursing or eating. When you think or feel it is a likely time for baby to eliminate, take her to the toilet place and give your signal. You will be amazed how quickly she learns to associate your signal with elimination, especially if you are consistent. Soon you can start getting her to go for you. The main types of signals that infants respond to are:

- vocal or verbal cues ("sssss" or "do you have to pee?")
- physical cues (in-arms position, location, receptacle, etc.)
- intuitive cues
- manual cues such as gestures or sign language

If you are consistent and fairly intense at first, your baby will associate your specific vocal, verbal and physical signals with toilet activity within a week or less. If it's time for her to go but there is no response to your signal, try running a little water in the sink or bathtub. The sound of running water may prompt her to go. You can also try running a little water over her feet, dipping her feet in water or sprinkling a little water on her tummy. If she still doesn't go, it means she doesn't need to go. Try again in 5–10 minutes or whenever her natural timing suggests.

In general, you should not have to signal baby for longer than 1–2 minutes. If there is no reaction, she probably doesn't need to go. Do not continue to hold baby in position unless she is comfy, happy, relaxed or wants to remain there. Sometimes she will want to remain in your arms longer, in which case you can continue trying to get her to go. If she resists and you cannot quickly distract and relax her, respect her wishes and try again later.

Many Westerners do not believe there is such a thing as telepathic communication between caregiver and child. Others believe this type of communication exists but that they are not able to achieve it. If you cannot relate to or experience this type of communication with your baby, don't worry about intuition for now. You can be just as responsive by using the other forms of communication.

If you feel that you are mainly guessing your baby's timing and that it is often merely a matter of luck if you get baby to go on cue, carry on using timing, patterns, baby body language, baby vocalizations and even "guessing." One day you may be surprised to suddenly hear or feel something that tells you, "It's time to pee her," and your intuition will kick in. If you ever all of a sudden think your baby might need to go, act on it rather than ignoring it, and you may be pleasantly surprised. After getting results this way, you may be able to supplement or change from relying on the clock to relying on intuitive timing.

Parents who feel they can communicate on an intuitive level with their babies can either purposefully direct specific thoughts towards their babies ("Do you have to pee?") from time to time or let the thought process flow, knowing that the right thoughts will go to baby at the right time. Intuition is a subliminal phenomenon that is always functioning in your subconscious. It is like DSL, constantly streaming in the background, and you just have to tap into the current to access it.

Mothers in so-called "primitive" cultures see baby as an extension of their own body. If you ask an Asian or African mother who uses infant potty training, "How do you know when your baby needs to go?" don't be surprised if her reply is that her intuition tells her. "I just know. Mothers just know." It's similar to knowing when your child needs to breastfeed—through various means, you learn and instinctively know when to offer the breast.

Manual cues are a form of sign language. Parent and child can define their own particular manual cues or use ASL (American Sign Language) or another sign language.

You can teach your baby to associate manual cues with elimination. This opens up a new and personal channel of communication. To make the ASL sign for "toilet," face your palm towards baby. Make a fist and place your thumb between your index and middle fingers (this forms the letter T for "toilet"). Then twist or shake your hand back and forth a few times to indicate "toilet action" such as, "Do you need to go?" or "Shall we use the toilet?"

Make your toilet sign when asking her if she needs to go, when seating her on the potty or toilet, and while she is peeing or pooing. Then expand the meaning. Reinforce the sign by saying "potty" or "toilet" while signing. Next, begin to sign as you point and walk towards the bathroom, toilet or potty. Then signal her in silence when you think she may need to go. Finally, sign your offer while in a different room.

Baby's Signals and Cues . . .

You'll need to learn to read your baby's cues and signals. You can do this by observing her natural timing and/or monitoring her body language and other cues. These cues may be audible, inaudible, visible or invisible. The main types of signals that babies send are:

- body language
- vocal cues
- intuitive cues
- manual cues such as gestures or sign language

Your baby makes facial expressions and uses other body language just prior to or while urinating or defecating. Through careful observation, you can learn to recognize your baby's toilet body language. For example, she may use her eyes to point towards the bathroom. If you are walking past her toilet place and she needs to go, she may lean or throw her weight in that direction. If she needs to poo, she might squirm as you walk past the bathroom. These are attempts to point before she can use her arm, hand and finger to point. Some body language is extremely subtle and hard to decipher. There are mothers who swear that their infants do not signal at all. If you are in this situation, use the other forms of communication for now, and watch for body language to become apparent as she matures. And be prepared for signals to change over time.

The list below contains examples of both spontaneous and learned body language signals. Your baby may use just one, a few or several or even her own unique cues not mentioned here.

Behavior:
- quieting: slows down or remains still and silent momentarily
- quick mood change from smiling and happy to grumpy or sullen
- stops or refuses to nurse, perhaps with a special "look"
- when in sling or other carrier, wriggles or kicks to get down
- suddenly stops or loses interest in activity (including babbling)
- hides or goes to private place to be alone
- undoes own clothing fasteners, removes diaper or undresses

Eyes:
- stares into the distance at nothing
- looks or stares at bathroom, potty or other toilet place

Face:
- pulls faces, grimaces, wrinkles face
- adopts a look of concentration or a blank, dreamy stare
- face turns red/flushes

Abdomen:
- tenses abdominal muscles
- contracts abdominal region when "pushing"

Whole Body (Physical):
- squirms, wriggles or twists body
- tenses or stiffens body
- shivers
- leans towards toilet place as you walk past it
- climbs into, or stands up in your arms or lap
- moves (scoots, wiggles, crawls or walks) towards toilet place

Legs:
- kicks or pumps one or both legs in the air (sometimes frantically)
- pushes against you with legs
- engages in unique leg position or movement

Breathing:
- changes rate of breathing
- takes a sudden deep breath
- breathes heavier or exhales loudly

Buttocks area:
- passes gas before defecation
- assumes special buttocks posture (newborns)
- pats diaper, butt or pants

Arms and Hands:
- points at or touches self, mother, toilet, potty, etc.
- uses sign language

Genitals:
- grabs or looks at crotch area
- points at, pats or pulls genitals
- penis/scrotum contracts or swells slightly before urination
- penis wiggles shortly before urination

The easiest cues to read are the vocal ones. For example, babies typically grunt before and/or during defecation. Infants also sometimes signal impending or completed elimination by way of other vocal sounds such as crying, yelling, squealing, gurgling, or breathing with a sigh or whimper.

Many mothers report that their babies send out pee signals on an intuitive level. The most common sensation is a feeling of spreading warmth, as if their babies were peeing on them. Others smell urine, hear the word "pee" in their minds or subtley feel a full bladder in their own bodies. But in all these situations, when they check their babies, they find that they are clean and dry! When the mothers then hold them in position to go, the babies respond by peeing. Some mothers report the same with defeca-tion—a warm sensation or the smell of baby poo precedes the actual movement. But not all babies communicate in this way. Some families report that their first child communicated intuitively while their second child did not.

Tuning in does not mean that all you think about is baby's elimination. It is an awareness in the back of your mind that your baby needs to go every once in a while. Watching for signals becomes second nature, and your conscious focus remains on other things most of the time. It is similar to breastfeeding on demand. You instinctively offer the breast when you know your baby wants to nurse. You do not watch her constantly for signs of being hungry, yet still you realize when she is.

A baby can start communicating to you with hand signals before she can speak. In comparison with the progress of learning a spoken language, sign language can be learned somewhat earlier in life, starting around 8.6 months.[1] If you frequently use a toilet hand signal with your baby, she will start using the signal early in life. At first it may be hard to distinguish an ASL "toilet wave" from a "bye-bye wave," but an attentive mother soon learns the difference.

Lois Baas (from video)

10-month-old graduate Zachary
making ASL sign for "toilet."

STEP 6: Understanding and Commitment

After you have tried and fully understood the first five steps of the in-arms phase, the next step is to determine whether or not you are prepared to do what it takes to move forward with this method of toilet learning. You'll need to make a further commitment and an increased investment of time if you decide to continue. From this point on, it will be necessary to observe and adhere to baby's natural rhythm whenever reasonably possible. If you do not have the opportunity to take baby to the toilet place throughout much of the day, strive to spend a minimum of one hour a day using this method, preferably at the same time everyday. Even if you can only concentrate on it in relation to a few feedings a day, this can keep baby's elimination awareness alive.

It may take several days or even a few weeks to be able to coordinate with your baby's timing and signals. It's fine to ease your way into this gradually. There is no hurry. It is going to take time and practice. Your confidence will build over time.

It is important to always remember that an infant will automatically urinate whenever her bladder is full. In no case should you direct anger at her if you arrive too late to take her to the toilet, nor should you feel guilty for not being on time. Both baby and caregiver need to be relaxed while using this natural method.

There is nothing complex or mysterious about infant pottying. This book contains a lot of information and tips. The idea is for you to pick and choose whatever helps and encourages both you and baby. *Whatever works best is the best approach.* And your approach will need to change over time, as your baby grows and changes.

Expectations

The goal of infant pottying isn't to speed toilet learning. A lot of parents start out expecting too much. Expecting too much too soon can lead to giving up. The best approach is to not have any time-critical expectations. Deadlines and expectations set us up for disappointment and feelings of failure if our child doesn't meet our arbitrary goals. In some situations, this leads to pressuring the child and ourselves and is thus counterproductive.

Of course, certain basic expectations must be in place before you begin, such as "infant pottying is possible," but aside from the obvious starting premises, it is unrealistic to expect anything specific at any stage. For example, no one should expect to get most pees and poos in the potty for many months. Likewise, newcomers may go days with few or no "catches." Infant potty training takes many months of practice to complete—in most cases, longer than a year—and there are plenty of rewards along the way. Some babies catch on quickly; others take longer, but they all make the journey at their own innate rate, and the best you can do is be there for them when they need you and when you are able to assist without yourself becoming too overwhelmed.

Each child is unique. There is no way to know at what age a child will be toilet trained or when a baby will begin to consciously signal her elimination needs. It is possible that she won't signal you until she is nearing completion of toilet training and that this might happen around the age of 24 months. If this is the case, you can use the other tools discussed in this chapter: timing, patterns and intuition. It doesn't matter how you figure out your baby's toilet times. The important point to remember is this: *If a child doesn't give clear signals, you can still move forward as a team.*

Parents who use this method can easily fall into the trap of being too hard on themselves. It's easy to feel like you have failed when you miss one or more pees or poos. If you reverse the way you view this *à la* "Is the glass half empty or half full?" it is easier to appreciate your efforts. If you catch just one or a few pees a day, don't be discouraged. Things will pick up in due course. Realistic expectations include an increase in communication, responsiveness, hygiene and bonding from the start, along with a gradual gaining of control over the months.

Take care that you do not become too obsessed with pottying. Keep a balance in your activities. If you get to the point that you feel you can hardly do anything else but potty your baby, you are trying too hard. If you find that you are constantly looking for signs and signals, or that you are imagining that every little movement or sound is a signal, you are overdoing it and headed for burnout. If you constantly worry about when you will finish, you will miss a lot of the "magic" and likely become frustrated. If you are thrilled at each little deposit in the potty and enjoying the closeness with your baby, you are gaining far more than potty progress.

Squirts and Spurts

Many infants urinate and defecate in 2–3 intermittent squirts and spurts. Once you're aware of this pattern, it's easy to notice. If possible, avoid diapering or dressing baby until she has truly finished going. If the wait between spurts is long and baby is impatient, take a short break, then bring her back to the sink, potty or other toilet place in time to complete elimination. If she has diarrhea, a cold or is suffering from another ailment, do not expect to capture all the spurts and squirts in a receptacle until she has recovered.

Diapers can accentuate squirts and spurts. This can be especially baffling for mothers who use a lot of diapers. It is not uncommon for a diapered baby to poo (or pee) a little, then hold back when she feels the sensation of excrement (or urine) against her body. Her mother dutifully changes the diaper, then soon finds poo in the clean diaper. She changes baby again, and shortly thereafter notices a familiar red-faced grimace or perhaps hears grunting or gas passing, and ends up with yet another poopy diaper. This cycle can continue through more changes. Babies (including newborns) who are allowed to eliminate freely into a receptacle sometimes learn to regulate their BMs within a few weeks or months, to the point that they have just one or two poos a day instead of a continual stream of small poops.

Accidents

Accidents are a normal part of infant pottying. Strive to transform any negative feelings about misses into a nonchalant and relaxed attitude. Do not assign blame to anyone, and do not feel guilty or that you are a failure if you are distracted and miss some signals. Bear in mind that some babies don't signal before every elimination and that others may not be signalers in infancy at all, in which case you can rely on elimination timing, patterns or your intuition. If you miss a pee or poo, clean up without emotion, move on and wait for the next moment to take baby to go. Become familiar with the various causes of your baby's accidents, and use this knowledge to reduce future misses.

If you or other family members feel stressed as a result of accidents, find ways to alleviate the tension. If you are worried about carpets, furniture or clothing, find a practical solution such as budgeting for carpet cleanings, protecting furniture with a cover, wearing casual clothing or using a diaper at times. If anyone in the household is squeamish about baby elimination, it may be helpful to know that infant pee is nearly sterile at the time of urination and that BMs from an exclusively breastfed infant are usually harmless if quickly cleaned up.

Once you start using this method on a regular basis, it will be tempting to try to impress friends and relatives by giving live demos with your adorable and amazing baby. You will soon learn that showing off is a no-no. Your baby is so in tune with you and her potty routine that she will sense a change or disruption in communication if you suddenly try to show her off to others. If she wakes up from a nap to find your guests oohing and aahing at her while you try to get her to pee for you, she is likely to be distracted by the people staring at her and lose her connection with you and her elimination functions. In short, it is generally best to keep toilet visits private and relaxed.

If you know your baby needs to go but she does not respond to your cues and instead pees the moment you finally lay her down, this could simply be due to her anatomy. The sphincter muscles automatically clamp shut when there is pressure on them. There is more pressure on the sphincters in an upright position, and when you lay your baby down, the muscles tend to relax and release the contents of the bladder. Try putting her down briefly to help her relax those muscles, then offer another pee opportunity.

Other causes of accidents, such as health or physical problems, becoming mobile and concentration on an activity, are discussed throughout this book, including the section on potty pauses and potty strikes. If you are still feeling uptight about accidents after reading this book, try to recondition yourself: Smile as you practice wiping up small puddles of water from the floor, until it becomes an automatic reaction and behavior on your part.

Changes in Timing

Sometimes due to illness, a change in diet, an emotional situation (arrival of a new baby, an upset in the home, etc.), travel, a change in routine (moving, hosting out-of-town guests, spending the night outside your home, etc.), milestones or any major life change, baby's elimination timing may fluctuate. Do not feel discouraged. A regular or recognizable rhythm will likely return once baby's situation is back to normal. The only time this will not be the case is when baby outgrows one pattern and adopts a new one. This, of course, will happen from time to time throughout infancy and toddlerhood. When this occurs, tune into your little one for clues, then observe and adjust to her new rhythms.

If you experience some difficult days, the best way to break through is to remain "cool, calm and collected"—don't let it get to you. Keep an even keel and you'll find your way. If you are feeling frustrated, angry or guilty, perhaps you are trying too hard. You may reach a plateau and feel "stuck" for a while. *The infant potty technique is not an exact science.* We adults tend to want things to progress logically and uninterrupted, but infant pottying moves more as a subtle ebb and flow where the tide is always slowly but surely advancing at its own unpredictable pace. It takes trial and error, and improves with experience and practice. If you try this with more than one child, you'll be more confident with the next.

Going Out Diaperless

Some mothers don't dare take their babies out diaperless, fearing embarrass-ing accidents. Going diaperless is a matter of preference and "what works best." If you are going out and she hasn't peed recently, potty your baby before departing. Offer her elimination opportunities at logical times when you are out. Devise a plan for finding toilet places, whether it be outdoors or in public facilities. Take your preferred equipment—a portable potty, child-size toilet seat or other device. Some mothers prefer to simply carry a diaper and hold their baby over the diaper at toilet times. Select whatever works best in a car, airplane, train or bus. If you are walking or cycling, become familiar with your surroundings so you can quickly find a toilet place. When pottying in shops or restaurants, you can seat your baby on the potty on top of the changing table or take your child-sized toilet seat along for use on the adult toilet. Your potty "route and routine" will soon become second nature and not require a lot of strategic planning.

Many mothers find that they are more attentive and more in tune with their babies when they go out—especially if wearing baby in a sling or other body car-rier—without the usual household distractions. On the other hand, there are mothers and babies who temporarily disconnect from their elimination awareness when they are out, due to involvement with their surroundings. If this proves to be the case for you, you may prefer to use diapers on outings, until you feel more confi-dent, tuned in and sure of yourself and your baby.

If you are using a sling and want to go diaperless but would like some extra security, place a diaper or soft cloth under baby in the sling. No matter how you are transporting baby, if so desired, it is fine for her to wear training pants or a diaper, either with or without a waterproof cover. The important thing is for you to feel relaxed and not worry about impending accidents, all the while being mindful of baby's elimination communication.

Dress for Success

Use clothing that is quickly and easily removable. Expect accidents and messes with whatever styles you use. The way you dress your baby is a matter of personal preference and a lifestyle choice and can range from naked to bare-bottomed, from training pants to diapers, from onesie or dress to stretchy shorts or pants with an elastic waist. To save money, consider visiting thrift shops and garage sales.

Climate and seasons are factors to be considered. Although easier to imple-ment in warm climates, IPT is used in all climates around the globe, including the coldest places on earth. Find ways to modify and adapt to your local weather. In a cold climate, wool knit pants with an elastic waist (and for pre-crawling babies, with enclosed feet) are warm and quick and easy to use. Specialized IPT clothing small enough to fit babies under 2 years is now available online from sites such as:

- weebees.com (cloth diapers, Chinese open pants and more)
- http://wonderbabydesigns.com (custom-made Poquito Pants)
- undiaper.com (training pants with an openable crotch)

Visit the Infant Potty Training Webring at www.timl.com/ipt to find the latest links for IPT clothing and cloth diapers, or use a search engine to find other sites.

Chapter 4
The Potty Phase

The potty phase begins when baby can sit comfortably on a potty or toilet—at first with moderate "loving live support" during the transition, then later on his own—and continues until he completes toilet learning. This chapter covers both:

- unstable sitters, for babies who cannot yet sit proficiently on their own and who need some physical support to steady them on the potty or toilet
- stable sitters

Unstable Sitters

Many parents start using a potty before their babies can sit well on their own. Since potties are generally designed for toddlers rather than infants, small babies may at first need support while they are on the potty. The coziest and safest way to assure baby remains comfortably and securely on the potty is to support him with your hands or arms and let him lean against your chest. This will keep him steady and secure, prevent him from falling in or off the potty and be reminiscent of the in-arms phase. It will also allow you to focus on him and notice the moment he eliminates.

It is not easy to find a potty that fits a tiny baby bottom since most potties are designed for bigger bottoms. Two brands that have models small enough for infants are BabyBjörn® and Graco. More models are available in Europe. If you use the toilet, BabyBjörn®, Flip-N-Flush, Graco, Cushie-Tushie and others sell attachable child-sized seats that fit dinky bottoms. You can find all these products online.

Small children sitting on a full-sized toilet, even one with a smaller seat attached, need constant supervision and companionship. If left alone, they could fall off or into the toilet. Most small children need help descending from the toilet when they are finished. A footstool can be helpful in this regard and also provide support for his feet while sitting on the toilet. Children unfamiliar with a toilet may at first fear that they will be flushed away. Others are frightened by the sound of the toilet flushing as they sit on it. Still others imagine that monsters or strange creatures live in a toilet and can attack them from behind, so to speak, until they grow accustomed to an adult toilet.

On the other hand, many children enjoy graduating to the big toilet that everyone else in the house uses. These children are usually content to use a detachable child-size toilet seat and enjoy flushing the toilet. An alternative use of the big toilet seat, especially for small children, is for the mother to sit on the toilet seat and hold baby in her lap, aiming baby so that his elimination goes directly into the toilet. This way he is sitting comfortably and securely on the big toilet, using mom as a warm cushion. A variation on the big toilet theme is for mom and baby to sit facing the back of the toilet, with baby seated comfortably on his mother's legs and between mother and the toilet tank. Some babies feel more secure facing the toilet tank rather than an open space at the front of the toilet. In addition, they can place a toy or book on the toilet tank. And as discussed earlier, another option is for the caregiver to hold baby in-arms while squatting in front of or standing over the toilet.

Babies typically graduate easily from the in-arms phase to a potty or toilet. The same basic method used during the in-arms phase works as you start the potty phase, the only changes being (a) a change in receptacle, (b) a change in position—sitting rather than in-arms squatting and (c) a possible change in location of the receptacle.

Make potty time as easy and simple as possible. Avoid clothing that will slow down the process. Buttons, snaps, buckles, zippers and tight-fitting outfits can cause delay and anticipatory accidents. The idea is for baby to be free to go as soon as you know it's time for him to go, or as soon as he signals you.

Find quick and easy ways to maintain good toilet hygiene. Never leave a small child alone at toilet time, as he may decide to sample his own excrement while you aren't looking.

As your baby becomes more aware of his environment and more able to explore his surroundings, he may at times be difficult to take to the potty or may forget to signal when he has to go—a situation that arises with most methods of toilet teaching. The solution is to stay connected, communicate, take him to the potty on time and be sure he is comfortable and relaxed. Use fun and creative ways to keep him seated long enough, while maintaining a balance between the following:

- Keep baby happy and entertained at potty time.
- Don't make unreasonable, ridiculous concessions or bribes to keep him on the potty or toilet.
- Don't require him to stay on the potty or toilet too long.

Since each parent-and-baby pair has different and individual needs, the more resourceful and creative you can be, the better. For example, during the transition-to-potty period, you may want to nurse your baby on or over the potty, just as you did during the in-arms phase.

Potty Comfort

Sitting on the potty or toilet should be as comfy as possible. Assess your overall situation and make any adjustments that will improve baby's comfort and level of contentment. If you live in a cold climate, for example, the awaiting potty or toilet seat is likely to be cold. Babies do not like being plopped onto a cold seat. This can cause them to dislike toilet time and rebel. Keep the potty or child's toilet seat near a source of heat such as a floor heating vent, or find another way to ensure that it is at body temperature or a little warmer. Other possibilities include placing a hot water bottle, heating pad, electric blanket, flannel diaper or other soft cloth on the potty. You can also warm it with your thigh, keep your hands between your baby and the cold seat, or hold baby in-arms above the seat.

For most, sitting on a potty is relaxing and comfortable. It is certainly easier—since it requires less pushing and straining—for a baby to poo into a potty or other receptacle than while sitting in a diaper seated on his rear end or while lying on his back or stomach. In addition, some mothers report that infant pottying relieves constipation and indigestion problems

An open-door policy helps children feel relaxed about visiting the potty or toilet. Familiarity with toilet use by others via live demos on the big toilet—dad for boys, mom for girls and siblings for siblings—creates a comfort level when small children are first introduced to the toilet. It is natural for children to want to imitate their older family members.

Stable Sitters

Once baby can sit steadily on his own, you no longer need to physically support him on the potty or toilet. Although he is becoming less dependent on you, your presence, commitment and care are still essential.

As he begins to walk on his own and gains more bladder and bowel control, one of the last aspects of the potty phase is for him to learn and remember to pull down his pants at potty time. This task, along with wiping, can require fairly sophisticated coordination, and these are often the last hurdles to attaining complete toilet independence.

Families living in warm climates, rural areas or the wilderness often let their babies remain bare-bottomed or naked during part or all of the day. They find it simplifies and speeds up toilet learning. For one thing, it eliminates the problems of dealing with fasteners and pulling pants up and down. Using IPT does not mean your baby has to run around naked. If you choose for your baby to be bare-bottomed, that is fine, but it is not a requirement for infant pottying.

Selecting a Potty

A potty should be of the correct dimensions to fit baby's anatomy. Bear in mind the following when making your selection:

- height
- seat diameter
- seat shape
- stability
- portability
- transparency

Most potties are designed for older and bigger children than your baby. His feet should rest squarely on the floor for comfort, support, security and extra pushing power. If his feet cannot reach the floor and his legs stick out straight, this position can eventually reduce or cut off the circulation to his legs and feet, causing discomfort or other problems. The weight of dangling feet and legs can cause his rectal muscles to tighten, making pooing difficult or even leading to constipation. Your baby should be able to sit down directly onto his potty, without using a step and without having to climb up onto it.

The seat should be of small diameter. Ideally, your child should be able to sit comfortably with a straight back at all times. Be certain that his buttocks does not sink into the potty, as this is not good for his spine and can be unhygienic. Smaller babies will need to be supported and held in place by their caregivers.

Boys require a potty with a small, raised lip at the front. When they pee while seated, they will "squirt" in unexpected directions without protection. The lip directs the pee into the potty. If you are ever caught in a situation where a lipped potty is not available, either you or the child can "aim" him in the right direction.

Although you are likely to at first support your baby on his potty, when he becomes more independent, he will start to find his way to the potty on his own.

Kevin Roberts

5-month-old Elsa enjoying near potty-sitting independence on the family bed, as she holds her mother's hand to the side. The built-in back support on the Graco potty helped support her before she could sit on her own.

Choose one that doesn't tip easily when he squirms. The BabyBjörn® Splash-Proof Potty is ideal for this, since the bottom edges extend out on the floor far enough so that baby's feet hold the potty in position. An added benefit is that when he stands up, the potty won't stick to his buttocks and then tip and spill.

A small, portable potty is very useful as you can take it with you wherever you go. If the potty you select is not portable and you must travel or be out of the house for some time, take along an attachable toilet seat or any sort of vessel that will serve the purpose.

A transparent or semitransparent potty is useful in that you know instantly when your child goes and can provide immediate feedback by praising him while he is going, or immediately thereafter. He is then free to leave the potty as soon as he is finished. This type of positive reinforcement encourages him to use the potty on a regular basis. If he has diarrhea, you will know not to let him get up right away and can tell or read him stories, play games or otherwise entertain him until he has finished tending to business.

If you can't find a transparent potty, another way to get instant feedback is to feel the bottom of the potty. It will change temperature when baby eliminates—unless you are in a very warm room or climate, or unless the potty is too thick to feel the warmth.

Potty Pauses and Potty Strikes

Some babies go on potty pause or potty strike. The main reasons for setbacks in IPT are usually developmental or emotional, when baby experiences distraction, intense learning, discomfort, upset or pressure (in these ways, a potty strike is similar to a nursing strike). More specifically, causes include developmental milestones and problems with health, family, physical comfort, daily routine or (breast)feeding. A potty pause is a temporary "phaseout" or hiatus from potty learning, while baby is working out an issue. It is not a conscious thing that a child does to be naughty or to manipulate you, whereas a potty strike can be a means of purposefully striking back at you for something that is bothering your little one. Strikes can last a day or longer, even up to a number of months, whereas pauses are usually less intense. In both cases, it is up to you to ascertain what is upsetting or distracting your baby.

Typical behavior for both potty pauses and strikes includes arching the back and straightening the legs, crying, screaming, holding back or refusing to sit on the potty. Note that these same behaviors can at times manifest for reasons other than a strike, such as misreading baby's signals or incorrect timing, in which case baby is simply letting you know he does not need to go potty. And be careful not to equate accidents with a potty strike—all babies experience numerous accidents during infant toilet learning.

The main reasons for potty pauses are:

- physical discomfort due to teething, illness, diarrhea or the need to pass gas
- developmental milestones (learning to crawl, walk or talk or mastering another major skill)
- temperamental reasons such as protesting the unwanted interruption of an activity, a change in schedule/routine or suddenly receiving less care and attention

If your baby is not feeling well, he might stop signaling and responding to your cues for as long as it takes for him to recover from his physical ailment. Viewed another way, infant communication can also help you find out about your baby's other needs. If he refuses to go on cue several times a day, this could be a sign that something is amiss, and you can look for ways to comfort him.

Diarrhea, the common cold and other illness can wreak havoc with pottying. Teething is another thing that can throw your baby off kilter and cause him to shut down for a while. With teething, there is the added complication that it may take days for you to even realize your baby is cutting teeth, plus babies cut lots of teeth over many months. If your child is not feeling well, he may need extra sympathy and understanding, and he is likely to lose interest in pottying for a while. Be sensitive to his needs. Do not view his refusals as rebellion or defiance. If you use force or punishment, it will backfire on you, and you could prolong the situation.

Developmental milestones tend to disrupt pottying for a number of reasons. Generally, as mobility begins to increase, so do accidents. Otherwise stated, during the learning of mobility, as mobility increases, bladder control decreases for a while. This is perfectly normal and to be expected. Some activities put pressure on the bladder, and this pressure can cause babies to unexpectedly pee. For example, when baby is creeping around on his belly during attempts to scoot or crawl, he tends to pee without warning. When learning to stand and walk, new sets of muscles are contracting in the back and abdominal regions, again pressuring the bladder.

With mobility come freedom and independence. Babies are fascinated by their surroundings, and some have such a love affair with all the new discoveries that they lose interest in pottying for weeks or months. In this situation, continue to offer opportunities to use the potty or toilet at times that do not upset your little one. If life is too stressful, it doesn't hurt to use diapers again for a while until the potty interest returns.

Learning the use and power of "no" is another milestone that can distract for a while. Children seem especially fascinated and empowered when they start signaling "no" or using the word "no." They like experimenting with the consequences. Sometimes it's possible to learn the difference between a negative no and an affirmative no, but be aware that the meaning can change over time. If need be, reduce peeing opportunities or take a break for some days or weeks until you find a more receptive time for your child.

When experiencing an "I'm busy learning something else" phase, a baby's "brain power" is temporarily diverted elsewhere. At this time, children have better things to do than deal with pottying. If you don't respect their "space" and determination, they can turn hostile in an effort to get you to back off for a while. In other words, adults can be the catalyst that turns a potty pause into a potty strike.

There are many other things that can cause a potty pause and/or lead to a strike. Travel, moving house, hosting overnight guests, divorce, quarreling or other tension in the household, arrival of a new baby in the family, adjusting to a new nanny or babysitter, switching from the family bed to his own bed and room, discomfort on a (new) potty or toilet, constipation, urinary track infections, dislike of a new toilet position or location, preference for one location only (perhaps in the bathroom where adults go), significant change in house temperature or noise level, construction in the house, receiving less care and attention (for example, at Christmas when you devote lots of time to shopping, cooking and guests)—all of these and more can trigger toileting trouble.

Strikes can start out for the same reasons as pauses but manifest themselves differently in that baby is sending an SOS message of discontent or disapproval and is awaiting resolution. If you are going through emotionally difficult times, your baby will sense this and may go on strike—a pee strike, poop strike or both. You might have to wait until you sort out your own problems before resuming pottying. On the other hand, solutions can seem amazingly simple once you figure things out. For example, you may be offering too many toilet opportunities in a quest for potty perfection. If so, repeat after me: "Reduce and relax!"

During a potty pause or strike, it is easy to mistakenly assume that baby has forgotten everything he once knew about toileting. This is not the case. Your baby is simply preoccupied and too busy doing other things—hence the term "potty pause." The best thing to do at this time is to either take a break for a day or longer and wait it out, or else cut down on potty visits and only make them at strategic times for a while.

Potty pauses and strikes are not unusual and should not discourage you from continuing. If after a sincere attempt you cannot find a cause, don't worry. Babies tend to advance and retreat as a part of normal development—three steps forward and a step or two back. Be patient as you wait for the synergy between you to return.

Definition of "Toilet Trained"

One of the most common questions asked about IPT is, "At what age will my baby be toilet trained?"

In one sense, Westerners do not consider a child to be toilet trained until he can perform all toilet functions independently, without reminders. This happens when a child knows and can remember where to find the potty or bathroom, walk to the potty or toilet on his own, pull down his pants without help, do the job, wipe, get off the potty, pull up his pants and remain dry all day and night. Seen in this light, a child would not be considered 100% toilet trained until his coordination is developed to such a degree that he needs no help locating and using the potty or toilet, and wiping and dressing himself.

In another sense, a child can be considered toilet trained at a much younger age, as long as you get him to the toilet on time and offer the obvious assistance. The basis of this is that baby has reasonable control over the sphincter muscles and understands the concept of going to a toilet place to eliminate but needs help and/or reminders to get there on time. While conducting extensive research on this method, I asked many IPT mothers to tell me at what age their children were toilet trained. The most common reply in Western countries was 12 to 18 months for reasonable daytime dryness. In Asia and Africa, most mothers will tell you their babies are toilet trained at 6 to 12 months of age. These claims of being "toilet trained" allow for the fact that baby is still partially dependent on someone to transport him on time to the toilet place.

Parental and cultural expectations must also be taken into account when considering the age of toilet readiness. Like many things in life, parental expectations can have both a positive and a negative effect on a child, depending on parental behavior. Encouragement and wishful thinking applied in a positive manner can lead to early development and early maturity in some physical skills. Where physical development is concerned, you're never expecting too much as long as you don't punish your baby for not living up to expectations. No feelings of disappointment, please!

In some areas of Africa, certain activities are prized, praised and encouraged from the very first weeks or months of life, activities that are not deemed nearly as important or that are considered impossible in early infancy by Westerners. These include sitting, smiling and toilet training. In rural Africa, babies are generally taught to sit and smile months before Western babies. Babies from several Asian and African societies learn and hone elimination skills in early infancy. The point is that if a behavior or skill is culturally important and encouraged by the parents, a baby is likely to be precocious in that behavior or skill when compared to babies who do not receive similar early teaching and opportunity for sufficient practice.

When Can Baby Be Diaperless?

There is no fixed time for this. The best time for your little one to start going diaperless is a matter of preference and of what is possible, practical and desirable with respect to your own individual situation. Being diaperless can be helpful or even indispensable for some, while for others it doesn't seem to make much difference. There are also mothers who feel tense and nervous if their babies are diaperless all the time. They constantly watch their babies and tend to interpret every little sound or body movement as a signal. In this situation, it is better to relax and use a diaper as a backup. The point is, the infant potty technique works with or without diapers, and many mothers use diapers in between potty visits.

As for when a baby is able to control his bladder and bowels enough to go diaperless, this again depends in large part on the parents' lifestyle as well as on the individual baby's physiology and stage of toilet learning. Some babies pee every 10 minutes while others pee every 3 hours, depending on the functional capacity of the bladder, infant age and intake of fluids. At age 4 months, some babies urinate every 2–3 hours and others still go every 10–15 minutes. At 6 months, some babies pee 6 times a day while others will void 20 times. Relatively frequent voiding is a normal condition for many and does not preclude going diaperless.

If you are worried about your carpets, one solution is to buy a fairly large, natural-fiber piece of remnant carpet and place it over your permanent carpeting. If your baby has accidents, you won't need to worry about your regular carpets. You can roll up the remnant whenever you like. If it starts to smell, let it air out in the sun.

The age range for totally ditching diapers can vary considerably. The important thing to bear in mind is that each baby is different. Some are easier to work with than others. Similarly, some mothers are more receptive, perceptive and able to open up than others. Every family situation varies and must be taken into consideration. Since there is no fixed length of time in which one should complete IPT, there are no feelings of failure. This method of toilet learning provides a means for you and your baby to function as a close and loving unit for however long it takes.

Chapter 5
Nighttime

Staying dry at night often takes longer to accomplish than staying dry during the day. The degree of difficulty of staying dry at night depends on your baby's elimination frequency and patterns, as well as on your diligence and ability to be in tune with your little one. At night, there is the added stress and complication of waking up from sleep, and the various aspects and consequences of this should be weighed and considered. It is important to do what seems best for both baby and the family as a whole.

Keep the bedding and clothing dry and clean, even if you have to change them at night. This encourages baby to remain dry. In the event of accidents, quietly and nonchalantly clean up, with as little fuss and disturbance as possible.

Many babies remain dry all night only to be left to wet their bed or diaper in the morning. Babies generally need to be taken to the toilet as soon as they wake up. Bear in mind that they often wake up before everyone else in the house. Remember to base the "first thing in the morning" pee on her timing rather than yours. If you do not take her to pee immediately upon waking, it will probably be difficult for her to wait more than 1 to 5 minutes before she goes. The result will be a wet bed or diaper, not because she wet it during the night but because no one made the effort to take her to pee when she woke up in the morning. As she grows and her bladder gains more capacity, she will be able to "hold it" somewhat longer after waking. Don't wait too long, though. Even most adults need to relieve themselves upon waking in the morning.

If you take baby to pee soon before she goes to sleep for the night and then get her to the toilet place when she wakes in the morning, there is a good chance she will stay dry all night. The reason baby can remain dry all night is because certain hormones cause urine production to decrease at night, so her kidneys produce less urine while she is asleep than during her waking, active hours. If you let her eat something with a high liquid content such as watermelon before bed, you can expect her to need to pee during the night. Babies who nurse or drink a lot before bed or during the night are also likely to pee once or even several times at night, especially when they are very young.

Bedwetting is fairly common among infants, and one solution is to pee them at night. How do you know when to pee your baby? Many stir, kick, cry or otherwise (partially) wake at night if they have to go. As with daytime signals, nighttime signals can be either blatant or subtle. Many babies are restless in their sleep. They might toss and turn, with or without sound effects such as grunting, or perhaps just turn their heads from side to side. They might roll over or raise their rear ends in the air in an attempt to get the pressure off their bladders. Mothers often assume that if babies wake at night, it is to nurse, and they quickly offer the breast. But many babies stir or wake at night to pee. Through observation, you will know if this is the case with yours. Some are adamant about fussing and waking you and will even refuse to nurse before they have relieved themselves. Others will eliminate then drift back to sleep without any nursing. And of course many will want to nurse themselves back to sleep after going.

But what if you aren't forewarned at night? Perhaps your baby doesn't squirm or wake before she pees. Maybe she went to bed hours before you, and you aren't present when she stirs or whimpers. Perhaps she just wakes up and lies quietly waiting. Or maybe she is a deep sleeper and sleeps through just about anything. If your baby wets the bed and you want to do something about it, figure out the optimal time to take her for a "preventive pee" at night and see if she will go for you.

You can let her go in a portable receptacle (bucket, potty, bowl, etc.) kept near the bed, or else take her to the sink, toilet or bathtub. You can also let her pee on a diaper, a cotton changing pad with a waterproof backing or anything else that works in your situation. A newborn can be placed on a diaper, towel, etc., on your chest or on the bed. After she pees, just toss the wet item into a container and replace it with dry one. As a general rule, do whatever is the least disruptive at night.

Keep baby warm and comfortable. Darkness or dim lights, silence or quiet surroundings, gentle and minimal movement or changing of clothing can all be helpful. Some babies only half wake up to go, keeping their eyes closed the whole time, then fall back into a deep sleep in your arms after peeing. If yours likes to wake up slowly, respect this tendency and let her wake at her own pace. But there is usually no need to fully wake baby or otherwise disturb her slumber. If she is awake after she goes, nurse her back to sleep. You may soon find that both you and your baby remain in a light stage of sleep while taking care of her nighttime toileting needs. Do whatever lets you both fall peacefully back to sleep.

Some babies respond well to your signals in the middle of the night while others do not like being moved or awakened to go. Nighttime pottying can be more difficult with deep sleepers in that it may be harder to elicit a pee on cue.

It can take a few nights to become accustomed to a nighttime routine and isn't unusual to meet with a little resistance at first. One mother discovered that candlelight mesmerizes and relaxes her baby—he stares at the glow, and out comes the pee. Try different strategies such as rocking baby in your arms, nursing her over a receptacle or nursing while walking around. Or it might be helpful to nurse her for a few minutes, then pee her and then nurse her back to sleep. After some nights, you'll get into a routine and will both grow accustomed to staying more relaxed during nighttime pottying. And of course things will change over time as your child physically matures and develops new habits.

Some parents find it easy to get up at night, while others find it extremely difficult. You'll soon ascertain whether or not it's a good idea for you and your baby to take her to pee at night. If you and baby don't find it too unsettling or tiring, carry on pottying at night. If it makes you negative or worn out during the day, or if disturbing your rest at night makes you susceptible to illness, it is better to sleep through the night. If your little one protests being pottied at night, it might be wise to "let sleeping babies lie" for some nights before trying again. If it goes well most of the time except for phases where her patterns change or when she is ill—she may temporarily nurse and pee a lot more at night—don't worry about getting up for every pee during that time. And always bear in mind that the infant potty technique is an ever-changing thing. Just when you think you have something figured out really well, your baby might transition to new timing, patterns and trends.

An important factor in the nighttime equation is clothing. Find something that is super fast and easy to remove with as little fuss as possible. A pajama top, long-sleeved T-shirt or sweater might be all you need for warmth. If diapering, fitted diapers are excellent in terms of keeping the bed dry.

But using diapers at night can actually encourage bedwetting, especially once a child has reasonable daytime control. This is particularly true with toddlers since having to remove a diaper adds to the time and complexity of using the potty or toilet independently, and this may be enough to discourage the attempt. Also, association with diaperlessness and/or the power of projection can have a positive effect on nighttime toileting with both infants and toddlers. One mother found that when her baby was diaperless at night, he remained dry, but whenever she diapered him at night, he wet the diaper. Once she noticed this pattern, she stopped diapering him at night. And let us not forget how disposables suppress feelings of wetness that might otherwise wake a child at night and encourage her to use the toilet or potty rather than her disposable diaper.

Diapers can be especially uncomfortable for boys. If your boy cries at night for no apparent reason, his discomfort could be caused by diapers restricting penis movement and swelling/expansion during a nighttime erection.

Once your child begins to walk, use one or more nightlights so she can see in the dark. Place the potty near the bed. Invite her to wake you when she has to go, even if you are co-sleeping. The thought of you waking up to accompany her might be just the encouragement she needs to get up at night.

If one parent remains at home with baby during the day, it is helpful if the other parent takes on the task of getting up at night whenever possible and reasonable. Some fathers are glad to make this sacrifice, while others flatly refuse to make the effort. Each family has to weigh their total situation in order to determine who does what, if anything, about nighttime pottying.

If you want your baby to be diaperless at night but are worried about your mattress and bedding, there are a number of ways to protect them. Natural wool is one of the best solutions since wool is resistant, doesn't grow bacteria or fungus, absorbs a lot of liquid before feeling wet and is a natural deodorizer. You can let baby sleep diaperless by placing a sheepskin rug (shorthaired is preferable, to reduce the risk of suffocation and also for cleaning purposes) or wool mattress pad under soft and natural material such as a cotton or flannel sheet. If the wool starts to smell after some days, let it air out in the sun. If you ever find mildew on the wool, thoroughly clean it asap. If you don't want to use wool, try cotton changing pads with an absorbent core and waterproof backing.

Some families don't worry about taking baby to pee at night. They figure that if they devote time to pottying during the day, they won't slow down the process by going off duty at night. Many families believe their baby will simply outgrow bedwetting.

If you are not getting up at night and baby pees most nights for a year or longer, it may be wise to reassess the situation and change tactics as a means to help her avoid long-term nocturnal enuresis (bedwetting at night after the age of 3 years). Enuresis is an elimination disorder that can last for years. In fact, adults in their twenties have been found to still be incontinent. There are a number of treatments available, but none are guaranteed to work. If your baby is showing repeated signs of enuresis, it might well be worth the sacrifice to get up at night and take her to pee, as a gentle and natural way to combat the problem before it progresses into a true elimination disorder.

Nighttime regression after staying dry for a month or longer can be caused by emotional factors. "Children's brain patterns change if they are overly tired, stressed, or depressed, preventing the sleeping brain from detecting signals from the bladder and awakening. The problem can be expected to disappear as soon as the child is back on an even keel. . . . Urinary tract infections, sleep apnea, diabetes mellitus, and seizure disorders can also cause sudden bouts of bedwetting. See your pediatrician if your child begins bedwetting after having remained dry for a month."[2]

Chapter 6
Late-Starters

This chapter is for parents starting with babies 6 months or older. By using a slightly modified version of this gentle method, it is possible to start late.

There is no clear cutoff age for starting the infant pottying method. Once babies pass the first window of opportunity around 4–5 months, some still remain receptive for a while. Others close down and then open up again, but there is no way to know when this might happen. And it is possible that some babies remain in a constant state of readiness. Their behavior might be mislabeled as "high needs," "colicky," "fussy" or something else. In the meantime, all they can do is await the day that their mothers finally respond to their toilet needs. It's not uncommon to hear the following, "My baby caught on within a few days!" Perhaps the same could have been said many months or even some years ago.

How to Start Late

If your baby is 6 months or older, you'll need to do two things: (1) Make some simple modifications to the infant potty technique and (2) add some traditional toilet teaching tactics to your approach. Most of the basic principles of infant toileting apply (it may be helpful to review Chapters 3–5), but you will need to find, sculpt and hone the best strategy or "recipe" for your child, family and situation. The following is a list of tips and guidelines, starting out with infant potty techniques, then blending into some mainstream conventional tactics that are often effective with toddlers. Some children catch on quickly while others take longer.

Parental Attitude

Be relaxed, gentle and patient. Accept and enjoy your child's learning pace. Avoid any and all pressure, anger, punishment and other negative emotions, words, intonation or actions.

Step 1: Choosing Your Basic Signal

Introduce a sound or word that you and your baby associate with elimination. The "sssss" sound is popular in many cultures, or you may prefer to simply say "pee pee" as your baby goes or when you think he needs to go. If he is in "mid-accident" and you are nearby, make the sound to help him learn the association between eliminating and the actual "stuff" that is coming out of him. You can use the same sound (or two different ones) for pee and poo.

Step 2: Timing and Elimination Patterns

Study your baby's elimination timing and patterns in relation to meals and awaking from sleep, then offer him chances to go at the most logical and obvious times. For example, most babies at first need to go immediately upon waking in the morning and after naps. Thereafter, they might need to pee, say, every 30–60 minutes two or three more times; then the timing may increase to an hour. On the other hand, some 6–9 month olds still pee at 15–20 minute intervals for a while. If your child is eating solids, he might need to go in the middle of a meal, immediately after the meal or 15–30 minutes after eating. Familiarization with these types of patterns can be helpful.

Step 3: Selecting a Location and/or Receptacle

If your baby is very small, you may want to start with in-arms pottying. But most late-starters are ready to sit on a potty or toilet. Where you keep the potty or potties is up to you. You can start out by keeping the potty in one place, although most find that moving it around as baby moves from room to room or else placing potties in different parts of the home allows quicker access and yields fewer accidents. Or you may prefer for your child to use the toilet. You can sit with him on the toilet, let him use a child's adapter seat that fits on the adult seat or simply let him sit independently while you keep an eye on him.

If you want your child to be diaperless between toilet visits, the best locations for this are outdoors in warm weather or else in rooms without carpeting. It is easier to detect and clean up after accidents if no carpets are involved.

Step 4: Positions

Try different potty positions until you find one that is comfortable and convenient for both you and your child. For smaller babies, you can try some of the in-arms positions that are used to hold infants. For more independent and mobile babies, in-arms positioning might not work. Look for a potty that fits your baby; otherwise, you can use the toilet, as described above. Boys often prefer to stand. Some children like to squat on the toilet seat.

Step 5: Signals and Cues

Study and learn your child's natural toileting body language. Each child has or learns his own set of signals. Some are extremely subtle and hard to recognize, while others may be obvious.

Try sign language or any hand signal you like. This is especially helpful with preverbal babies as it enables them to communicate their needs before they can speak. Once a baby starts to utter deliberate sounds and words, add verbal communication to your list of signals to notice. And remember that your child may at first use the word "pee" for both pee and poo (or vice versa) and/or announce the need to go "after the fact."

Step 6: Understanding and Commitment

Once you have a good understanding of how infant pottying works, you are at an important crossroads. If you would like to continue, you'll need to make a further commitment about devoting time to your child's "pot luck." Try it for a few weeks, then assess if you want to continue.

If your baby catches on quickly, it will encourage you to continue. If you get no results after 2–4 weeks, you can either simply carry on or else take a break and try again in 2–4 weeks. Even if your child doesn't appear to know what is going on, it is fine to still potty him as long as you are both happy and comfortable with it. Some toddlers develop considerable sphincter control rather suddenly, within just a few days or weeks, but it's not possible to know beforehand if or when this might happen. Also bear in mind that the more potty practice your toddler gets, the sooner he is likely to gain control of his sphincters and master his toileting skills.

Even if you find it is too much for you and give up at some point, your efforts will not have been in vain. Research has shown that many children retain some potty learning, even if their parents give up at some stage, and that it manifests itself later. Toddler toilet teaching tends to be faster and easier with children who had some experience with infant elimination training.[3]

Clothing

Try to "dump diapers" altogether or as often as possible to help your child unlearn earlier conditioning. This does not mean that you let your child pee and poo all over your house. Use common sense! Although it is not a requirement for babies to be bare-bottomed, it heightens their awareness of elimination and speeds up the learning process (sometimes dramatically). They instantly experience cause and effect. Find a way to work some diaperless hours into your day, when convenient and the least likely to cause stress. For example, if you are going diaperless at home, to avoid worry, you may want to use diapers as a backup when going out.

If you are using disposables, try switching to cloth diapers at least part time. With cloth diapers and no plastic cover, you know immediately when your baby goes. You can thus start to learn and recognize elimination timing and patterns. At the same time, you can change your baby as soon as he goes and avoid encouraging or teaching him to be comfortable with wetness.

Try a pair of training pants, and if they do the trick, invest in more. They are far easier than diapers to pull up and down. In addition, they soak up minor elimination dribbles and protect your busy baby's bottom and genitals.

If your baby seems ready, try regular undies. Pretty undies might be the catalyst that motivates a girl to stay clean and dry. Boys might be inspired to keep their favorite undies dry.

Use easy-to-remove pants. You can sew your own little shorts and pants, using pajama bottoms or sweat pants with an elastic waist as a basic pattern. These are easy to pull up and down in a hurry. Use any material(s) you like, based on comfort, climatic conditions, budget considerations and any other relevant factors.

Chinese open-crotch clothing might work for you. They enable babies to squat-and-go (or sit-and-go) without wetting or soiling themselves. This reduces the worry about dressing and undressing and cuts down on toileting delays and accidents. In cold weather, Chinese pants can be made of warmer materials.

Combining Infant & Conventional Techniques

Tactics . . .

- Make potty time fun time. Read books with your child, including books on potty training. Let him play with a favorite toy.
- If or when your child is old enough to care, take him shopping and let him help select a potty. By being involved this way, he is more likely to want to use the potty.
- Use an open-door policy by letting your baby accompany you, dad (fathers are especially helpful with boys) or siblings to the toilet. Let baby observe you and/or other family member(s) using the toilet and talk to him about using the potty or the toilet with a child seat attached. Learning by example and observation can be helpful for many, but don't make a big deal out of it. If your child is curious, he will observe and learn.
- With boys, try target practice by having your son aim at something floating in the toilet (examples: Cheerios, bits of toilet paper or store-bought targets designed for this purpose) or outdoors at his favorite target (example: a tree or a rock, perhaps with an actual target on them). He can also have fun drawing patterns in the dirt or snow, playing pee games such as seeing who can shoot farther, or crisscrossing streams with dad or a brother.
- Concerning praise, do whatever feels right, normal and natural for you and your little one. If you feel like praising your child, fine. If you don't believe in praise, simply state or explain what is happening when your baby goes for you.
- Use trial and error to find what works for you, always remembering that each child and each family situation varies from the next.
- If your child resists the potty or toilet, try to calm and relax him (example: give him something to drink), then offer again.
- For parents starting with children who are already walking, any time your toddler goes on the floor or in his clothing, tell him matter-of-factly what he did and then tell him that it belongs in the potty. Clean the mess and, together with your toddler, take it to the potty, toilet, hamper or laundry room. Explain again that it is best for the pee and poo to go in the potty or toilet. Do this each time he has an accident.
- Expect some resistance and fooling around by toddlers. For example, when they go through the phase of saying "no" to everything, their "no" does not always really mean "no." In short, if you ask your toddler if he needs to go potty and are met with a resounding "no," this response may sometimes have little to do with your question. This is all part of learning to understand your child's communication.
- Answer any and all questions your child may have about toileting, even if you've already explained the same thing many times.
- Sometimes offering a choice works well. If your toddler is squirming or holding himself, or you otherwise simply know it's time for him to go, ask if he would like to go and use the potty or if you can bring it to him.

- Constantly explain what is going on and what you are doing. Try to engage your child in the conversation by asking questions, "Are you telling me you need to go? Do you need to go? Shall we try the potty?" Or if he is in a no-to-everything stage or mood, adopt a "don't ask, do tell" approach, "I think you have to pee. Let's go read a book together while you try."
- If your child dislikes reminders or talking about toileting, don't say anything at all about pee, poo, the potty or the toilet. Every hour or so comment out loud (so he can hear) that you really need to go to the toilet, and then go there. If he follows you and one day uses his potty, don't comment or praise him unless you feel he will be open to this.
- Consult parenting books and look for more ideas. Read through the positive tips and advice offered for conventional training and test some of these approaches to see if they work with your child.

Siblings . . .

- Siblings can be a great help. They can teach by example, inspire, entertain and assist in many ways. Some siblings are better at "reading" their baby brothers or sisters than adults.
- Many families who learn about this method a little late end up potty training two children at once: twins, a baby and a toddler, or even two toddlers. Parents with two small children can teach both children simultaneously, as long as you are patient; don't have expectations that could lead to negative feelings or reactions; and respect/accept their individual rates of development.

Pace . . .

- There will be good days and bad days, amazing successes and the inevitable setbacks. Expect one step back for every three steps forward. Small children are very busy learning many new skills and achieving milestones, as well as going through some occasional discomfort such as when they are teething or ill. Many things (including travel or guests) can interrupt their potty learning on a temporary basis, but they will get back on track if you hang in there.
- Do not expect immediate or clear-cut results for several months. There is no fixed time scale for learning. Many parents feel frustrated if their baby doesn't seem to care about staying dry, forgetting that they taught him to pee in a diaper in the first place. It takes most babies considerable time to unlearn this. Give yours a while to make the connection and transition.
- Never compare your child's results with another in a competitive or judgmental way.
- Some parents have no trouble getting their baby to pee in the potty but reap no results for quite sometime with poos, or vice versa. Don't worry! This too shall pass.
- Go with the flow of your baby's natural learning process. A common scenario at first is for toddlers to let you know they peed or pooed after they have gone in their pants or diaper. This is part of the learning process, and your child will eventually learn to inform you beforehand.

Attitude . . .

- Be positive—never negative, punitive or coercive. Do not pressure your child.
- If you feel elimination is "yucky" (a Western sentiment or hang-up, stemming in large part from having to come into contact with waste when changing or cleaning diapers), strive to get over this feeling. This is where kids gain control or get stubborn, if they know it bothers you. In many non-Western societies, mothers just smile at accidents and clean up, with no negative emotional reaction.
- Listen to the voice within, trust your intuition, have faith in yourself, relax and enjoy.
- Be creative. Adopt the motto "Whatever Works" and proceed with an open mind.

Hurdles You May Encounter

It is usually (but not always) harder to start with a mobile baby who has been "trained" to go in a diaper or who wears disposables and does not associate the feeling of wetness with elimination. Here is a summary of the main reasons it can be difficult to begin at 6 months and older:

- Baby has been trained to go in a diaper.
- Baby has lost awareness of the elimination functions.
- Parents were not responsive to elimination communication in first sensitive period.
- Baby has developed an ego and a will of his own.
- Baby is mobile and active. When he learns to crawl and/or walk, he will naturally want to explore his surroundings, to play and focus his attention on new and exciting things. If he is not accustomed to spending time at potty sessions and if he is not aware of his "toilet muscles," he is not likely to understand why he is being detained on a potty and is thus not likely to want to remain there.

It's Your Choice!

Clearly, parents should be able to make a personal and informed decision about their preferred method of toilet teaching, and honest and adequate information should be readily available for these purposes. As stated earlier, no one claims that the infant potty technique is the right method for all families, but it is definitely the best method for many.

If you prefer to give your baby the option to go in a toilet, potty or other receptacle rather than in his clothing, more power to you. If you like the idea of baby going diaperless part time or even full time and would rather use a diaper on the floor than on your child for the occasional accident, or if you'd rather clean up occasional accidents than struggle over diapering, go for it!

Chapter 7
Medical Opinions & Anatomy

Although infant elimination training is not well known in the USA, there are some doctors and pediatricians who are supportive. They have for the most part traveled abroad and witnessed it firsthand, had personal contact with experienced parents or else are (spouses of) immigrants who grew up in cultures where this method is used. This chapter discusses favorable medical opinions and findings, and the basic physiology and anatomy.

Perspectives from East Africa: Three Studies

Marten deVries, MD, found that babies of the Digo tribe in Kenya start elimination training at 2 to 3 weeks of age and attain reasonable night and day dryness by the age of 4 to 6 months. The results of this study were published in *Pediatrics* and contradict and disprove the claim by Western medicine that babies have no control of the sphincters and other muscles needed for elimination until 18 months to 2 or 3 years of age.

There is a stark contrast between the experience of the people of East Africa and the view of Western medicine. One of the most famous child-raising experts of our times, T. Berry Brazelton, bases his child-oriented approach to toilet training in large part on maturational readiness. Brazelton advises parents to be patient and wait until their children take the initiative to start toilet training toward the end of the 2nd year. In Africa, the Digo and many other peoples and tribes place importance on infant toilet training. In their experience, muscular and neurological development as defined or limited by current Western medicine are not an issue. They believe and know firsthand that infant elimination training is effective.

Dr. deVries points out that cultural differences in the initiation and method of infant elimination training are related to different expectations of infant capabilities and performance. His article discusses a "cultural blueprint" for child-rearing behavior. "A network of complexly related factors shapes a culture's ideas of what infants are and what they can do. Training behavior is carried out in light of these expectations."

DeVries concludes his *Pediatrics* article by urging pediatricians to be flexible in family guidance. He stresses that child experts should take the overall setting into account, including cultural values and infant needs. "By dogmatically advocating a seemingly scientific approach while ignoring the potential diversity and effect of maternal and family expectation, the clinician may, in fact, thwart the training goals." He suggests that further research into this topic will one day yield valuable therapeutic results.[4]

Mary Ainsworth dedicated 11 pages to infant elimination practices and training in her book *Infancy in Uganda*. She reported that in the past, the Baganda infants of Buganda, Uganda, traditionally began elimination training around 2½–3 months. Training is still begun at or before the age of 4 months, sometimes as early as 1 month old and in most cases is done consistently and conscientiously. Success is dependent upon close interaction with babies; more specifically, it is contingent upon the baby giving recognizable signals and the mother's timely response

3-month-old Digo (Kenya) baby in
standard urination training position:
before, during and after.

Mother makes "shuus" sound to
elicit urination.

Baby and mother both look satisfied
after the fact (1977).

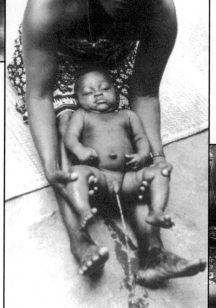

Marten deVries (all)

Epelboin/CNRS

A mother in Ibel, Senegal, using classic toilet training position.
Child sits on mother's upturned feet while waiting to go (1990).

Epelboin/CNRS

18-month-old Senegalese in her communal home.
For now, privacy is not an issue (Malicka, Senegal, 2001).

to them. There were some situations where elimination training took longer than
the norms given here, but in such cases, the mother was either not present when
needed or failed to pay adequate attention to her baby's signals.

The range of ages at which soiling the bed ceased was from 5–11 months; in
addition, mothers whose children were trained before Ainsworth arrived claimed
their babies finished this phase at 4–8 months. Bedwetting ceased between 9 and
22 months of age.

Soiling the house generally stopped between 8 and 12 months of age (a few
took up to 20–22 months), at which time most of the babies were able to go outside on their own initiative when they needed to defecate. The age for ending urinating indoors was just under 12 months. Ainsworth concluded that Baganda elimination training is at least as effective as the training methods used in Western
cultures.[5]

In her ethno-psychological study of African children, Marcelle Geber observed that Ugandan mothers were attentive to all the needs of their infants, including elimination cleanliness. She noted that Ugandan mothers carrying their babies on their backs were never urinated or defecated on by their babies and that their babies were always clean in this regard. When babies were old enough to walk, she observed them going outdoors, without prompting, to relieve themselves. Geber reported that Ugandan children completed toilet training between 15 and 24 months.[6]

Favorable Western Medical Opinions

1971 – Report by Thomas Ball, Ph.D.

Thomas Ball found that the infant potty technique can be interpreted within the framework of operant conditioning as "toilet training by reflex. The baby does not get used to eliminating in his diaper and does not feel comfortable doing so, [and] therefore will fuss to have the potty placed on his buttocks."

Thomas based his findings on research conducted by Mrs. Lela Humphries who devised her own infant potty learning approach for catching BMs and used it with her three children who were born between 1947 and 1956. She stated that while she was feeding her first son, she noticed that each time he had a bowel movement it was during a feeding. "I could always tell by the facial expression when the movements were going to occur." At 6 weeks of age, she would unpin the left side of his diaper, and the instant he made his facial expression indicating an impending BM, she would pull the diaper to one side (without actually taking it off), place the potty between her legs and place his buttocks on it. She left the diaper draped over his front in case he peed. "His position was the same as if he did not have the pot under him. He did not make any kind of fuss." She reported that her first two sons completed bowel training reasonably well at age 6 months and bladder control around the age of 14 months.

Her third son had Down's syndrome, but this didn't deter her. Although she kept no records, she recalled that he would scoot to the bathroom door and whine to be put on the potty before he could walk, and that at 16 months he started walking and would head to the bathroom when he had to go.[7]

1978 – Comments by Gersch & Ravindranathan, MDs

Two doctors endorsed the deVries Digo study via letters to *Pediatrics*. Marvin Gersch wrote that the merits of the deVries article demonstrate, among other things, that "our previous thoughts of toilet training were incorrect; training can be accomplished and has been accomplished at a much earlier age."[8] S. Ravindranathan also sanctioned the observations and conclusions of deVries when he wrote, "Not only does this bring about closer mother-infant interactions, contact, and communication, but it also eliminates future attempts at unnecessary coercive methods on a reluctant toddler."[9]

1985 – Study by Paul Smeets (Professor of Psychology) et al.

In this study, three girls and one boy started between the ages of 3–6 months. The parents used part-time toilet learning, spending 3–4.5 hours a day (but not every day of the week). To get the attention of the baby, the parent held or tapped the potty, or else called or touched the child while holding or tapping the potty, in order to be sure the baby looked at the potty before being placed on it. If the baby went within about 3 minutes, the adult displayed pleasure and approval; otherwise, the baby was removed from the potty. This phase of the study was completed when a baby had at least 18 BMs on the potty plus 8 out of 10 consecutive training days without any bowel accidents.

The next phase established a relationship between potty reaching/grabbing and both types of elimination. The potty was located 30 cm from and slightly to the right front of the baby. Upon spontaneously signaling or reaching for the potty or else when the mother knew it was time to go, the baby was guided to grab the potty and then sit on it.

All four babies completed training before they could walk, between the ages of 8.5–10.7 months. However, the endpoints or definition of completion here would not be acceptable to all Western families since "At the end of the program, the babies were not yet required to hold their eliminations longer than a few minutes and still needed assistance on taking the appropriate position and dressing and undressing."

The study reaches the conclusion that "the maturational explanation for the success of currently advocated delayed training methods should be reconsidered."[10]

1990 – Commentary by Paul Fischer, MD

Fischer debunks the American view that a child must be both "psychologically and physiologically 'mature' before successful toilet training can occur. . . . There has been almost no research to document these theories. They are no doubt nonsensical to much of the world where 'potty training' begins shortly after birth."

Dr. Fischer's Pakistani wife and mother-in-law started infant pottying with their 2-week-old daughter and reported that by age 3 months, she "obviously understood the association of the time, sound, and body position with voiding and defecation. By 1 year of age she was out of diapers both during the day and at night."

He states that people in much of Asia and Africa find the Western version of toilet training to be "primitive and unsanitary." Concerning the premise that infant potty training can lead to psychological problems, he states, "I can only speculate that this stems from attempts to use negative reinforcement with 18-month-old children who have had no prior conditioning. This is certainly not the case for the millions of children around the world who are trained in the first year of life."[11]

1993 – Interview with Dr. Leah Lamb, Pediatrician

Dr. Leah Lamb, pediatrician, has closely watched many women in India and North Africa complete infant potty training. She states that it takes a special kind of mother to bond closely enough and pay special attention to her baby's signals in order for the training to be successful. "This is a really gentle method, a mother-child dyad, bonded interaction. The parent/caregiver works with the baby, listening to his cues and signals. It's gentle and it's kind. I don't see that it would have any negative effect on an infant at all.

"Basically, the child is responding to behavioral conditioning. The sound that the mother makes, coupled with her being in tune with the baby's signals, will result in the child either urinating or defecating on cue.

"Infant potty training is not the old militant-style toilet training of the West. Instead, it is a method where the mother is responding and tuned into her baby's internal, physiologic schedule, and the child has assistance and an advocate who helps him accomplish going to the bathroom. You're not expecting a child to do it on his own early in the process.

"This is an interactive process between a mother, or a father, and a baby. The parents have to be involved and bonded enough to the baby in order to correctly pick up and act on his signals.

"Traditionally in Western AMA thinking, a child really doesn't have, as they say, the ability to respond. We physicians are taught that the neural maturation that allows for complete toilet training occurs somewhere around the age of 2 years. However, if the child is tuned in and sensitive to prompts in a nonpunitive way, he will respond. It's behavioral conditioning, and the child will 'go' for you.

"This method is about a parent and a child interacting and accomplishing a task together. In Western culture, we separate our children from us. We don't sleep in the same room with them, and there is much more emphasis on individuation and privacy. The child is seen as a separate entity. With this infant toilet training method, you're going back to a more natural state where the mother and child are as one unit, where they are interrelating with each other."[12]

1997 – Book by Charles E. Schaefer, MD

In his book *Toilet Training without Tears*, Dr. Schaefer discusses various methods of toilet training, including what he calls the "early approach" for babies between 3–15 months of age. He reintroduces the method of toilet training used in the USA in the 1920s and 1930s, noting that this was a conditioning process based on learning by association. In addition, he emphasizes that child development experts and pediatricians of the day coerced parents into adopting the wrong parental attitude and that this is what has given early toilet training a reputation for being harsh, rigid and punitive. Schaefer advocates a positive and unemotional attitude as well as a nonpunitive and non-coercive approach. After years of analytic and cross-cultural studies, "we now know that the age at which a child is trained is not the cause of later emotional and psychological problems; rather, it is the parental attitude that is used during the training period that will determine the long-term effect of toilet training."

Schaefer also gives infants credit for having some ability to control elimination. "Although it is not known exactly when a child can attain this kind of muscular control, studies have shown that some infants between three and six months can learn this skill very successfully, provided their caregiver is observant of the signs that indicate a need to eliminate and then acts promptly to put the child on the potty." He also says that babies are able to gain complete voluntary bladder and bowel control starting around the age of 15 months or later and that it is unrealistic to expect complete control before this time.[13]

1999 – Comments by Altemeier & Hemme, MDs

In *Pediatric Anals*, William Altemeier, MD, and Cheryl Hemme, MD, give credence to infant toilet learning. "There is little question that children can be toilet trained by 1 year of age." They qualify this statement with an emphasis on taking a relaxed approach, as they "remind parents that we all pass through these development phases, so relax and enjoy the ride." They also warn that "diaper changing in day care does have infectious risks."[14]

2000 – Study by Bakker & Wyndaele

Physiotherapist E. Bakker and urologist Jean-Jacques Wyndaele of University Hospital Antwerpen conducted a study to "evaluate changes in the onset of toilet training, the attitudes of parents and the results of training during the last 60 years in Belgium." Their findings indicate that voiding problems have increased in recent years and suggest that a major change in the way parents now toilet train their children compared with the approach used 60 years ago may contribute to the apparent increase in lower urinary tract dysfunction among children.

"Most authors are convinced that the development of bladder and bowel control is a maturational process which cannot be accelerated by toilet training." But their findings contradict this theory, instead indicating that "the age at which bladder and bowel control were achieved showed the same differences among the groups as the ages at the onset of training."[15]

2000 – Comments by Dr. Lauri Nandyal

Dr. Lauri Nandyal discounts claims of psychological damage resulting from infant potty teamwork and states that these claims refer to a very different method of toilet training. She calls the current Western medical views on maturational readiness "medlore" which is based on opinion and commercialism rather than scientific proof. She explains her conclusions in her testimonial ("A Physician Speaks Out") at the start of Chapter 10, where she recounts her personal experience using infant toileting with her third daughter.[16]

2000 – Video by Dr. Barbara Gablehouse, Pediatrician

In her video *The Potty Project*, Dr. Barbara Gablehouse states that 85 percent of the world's babies are toilet trained by 1 year of age and stresses that those babies "have the same muscles and the same ability to control those muscles as our [Western] babies. We simply need to give our babies the opportunity to practice this skill." She compares toilet learning with the learning of other important developmental skills such as walking and talking. A baby needs to incrementally learn a variety of related skills over time, such as balancing, standing, stumbling and taking steps, before he can walk, and if parents help and encourage him, he learns faster and easier. In the same way, a baby needs practice, positive reinforcement and time to gain control of his bladder and bowels. "Like all of your baby's learning, repetition is crucial for successful early toilet learning. . . Your baby will master toilet training by repeated opportunities to practice."[17]

The Potty Project is aimed at a mainstream parenting audience. It includes some shots of babies using a small child's seat on the toilet but does not show any in-arms positioning or use of potties or other receptacles. One of the strong points is that the video and study were organized by a board certified pediatrician. This can be helpful to AP and other families into alternative parenting styles, in that the video might help convince skeptical and unsupportive relatives and friends to be more accepting of IPT.

2002 – Commentary by Dr. Linda Sonna, Psychologist

"Child development experts in the U.S. continued to push back the recommended age for beginning toilet training since the turn of the 20th century, when the custom was to begin around age two to three months. A dramatic change came with the simultaneous introduction of disposable diapers in the early 1960s and the dissemination of renowned author/pediatrician T. Berry Brazelton's 'later-is-better approach' to toilet training. Brazelton warned that to begin before children had achieved adequate sphincter control was likely to create psychological difficulties that might well translate into a significant delay in skill acquisition, and he attributed chronic problems with bedwetting to premature training efforts." Dr. Sonna has not found any evidence to support these claims. "While some children do self-train virtually overnight if nothing is done until close to age three, habits of wetting and soiling are well entrenched by then, and many youngsters require a lot of time and have considerable difficulty. It is no longer unusual for children age four to still be in diapers.

"As a result of all of the warnings about the need for toddler readiness, the myth that younger toddlers (and some older ones) lack sphincter control began winding its way through the pediatric community. Amazingly, the knowledge that infants in fact have sphincter control was lost in two short generations. When American parents are informed that many foreign babies are routinely trained at younger ages, their first response is to deny that such a feat could be possible. Their second is to insist the training methods must be harsh and cruel. They cling to that notion even after hearing descriptions of the actual methods parents use."[18]

2002 – Commentary by Dr. Simone Rugolotto, Pediatrician

Dr. Rugolotto, pediatrician and neonatologist at the University of Verona, Italy, has personal experience with infant elimination training: He and his wife are raising their son using this method. Dr. Rugolotto states that the fact that early infant toilet training is a common practice in Asia and Africa "shows that toilet training in early infancy is possible and without major side effects. Babies can clearly communicate their needs, and we can help them to eliminate in a gentle way, by bringing them to the bathroom and using a potty, in a more natural and comfortable manner than eliminating in a horizontal position into a diaper. Babies do have control over their bladder and bowel functions; otherwise they would eliminate feces and urine continually, which obviously does not happen. More particularly, the elimination process is an active one, and we can see all the efforts made by infants during this activity. When they are not able to retain feces and urine any longer, they feel discomfort, give signals (e.g., cry), and, if no-body helps them, they let the process happen in their diapers.

"Infant toilet training has many advantages and should be supported by current pediatric knowledge. Some of the advantages are the following: an easier approach to 'voluntary' toilet training during childhood (children will accept the potty more easily than children who have never used it before); less cutaneous rash (due to less contact between feces or urine and skin); and a closer bond and better understanding between mothers and their children (when effective attention is given to a specific need instead of the usual pacifier or bottle). We are not aware of any side effects of early toilet training. No evidence-based medicine is available on this topic. Unfortunately, no randomized controlled studies have been done on early-versus-late toilet training, and I hope that in a few years some will be performed to give a new option to children and parents."[19]

Anatomy

Urination and defecation involve the use of both voluntary and involuntary muscles. As the name suggests, "voluntary" muscles are those over which we have conscious control, while "involuntary" muscles are not under our conscious control.

A child who begins toilet training in infancy can learn to control the voluntary muscles of the urinary bladder and bowels at the earliest moment possible. By the time he gains full control of these muscles, he is thoroughly acquainted with a grown-up toilet routine.

The main muscles involved in going to the toilet are the sphincter muscles. These help control both the bowels and bladder. They are circular muscles that constrict an orifice. In a normal contracted condition, they hold the orifice closed. In order to allow the orifice to open, the sphincter muscles must relax.

Doctors and medical books in Western countries typically state that the sphincter muscles mature between 20 and 24 months of age. It is mainly on this basis that they dismiss the concept of starting potty training before 1 or even 2 years of age. What they fail to mention, however, is that their 20-to-24-month figure represents the extreme—the longest time it takes for these muscles to fully mature—rather

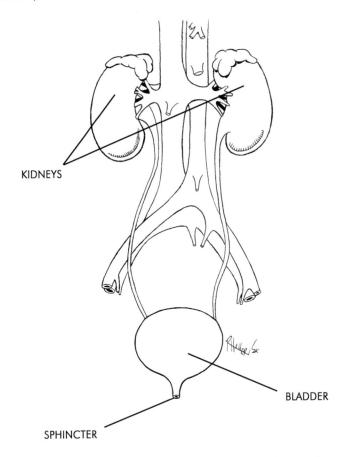

KIDNEYS

BLADDER

SPHINCTER

than the average. They do not take into account the many babies whose muscles develop before 20–24 months. They do not consider the fact that infants are able to release urine and bowel movements upon association with a signal to release. Likewise, they fail to consider societal factors such as acculturation, support, parental devotion and lifestyle choices.

A more accurate statement is that with regular practice, the sphincter muscles can complete development between 12 and 24 months of age, with 18 months being the average age at which a baby can be potty trained reasonably well but still needing to be reminded at times, with only occasional accidents. As with everything in life, there are always exceptions to the rule. Some babies gain complete control before 12 months of age, while others may take longer than 24 months.[20]

There is another equally disturbing problem with the current Western medical philosophy of potty training. The premise that a child cannot control urine or bowel movements until a minimum of 20–24 months of age implies that a baby lacks any muscular control of his bowels and bladder before that time. The very first time your infant responds to your cue to pee or poo, you will prove this theory wrong and see that your infant does indeed have some control over his "toilet muscles."

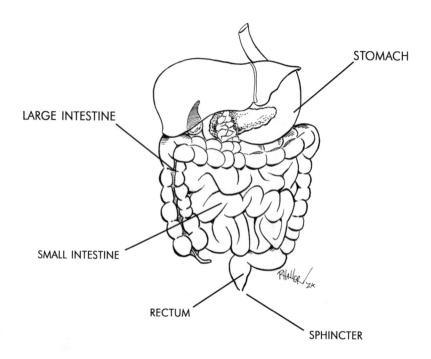

STOMACH

LARGE INTESTINE

SMALL INTESTINE

RECTUM

SPHINCTER

Even if it turns out that your child develops complete control over the sphincter muscles at a relatively late age (2½ years or older), infant pottying will still prove a positive and useful experience in many ways. For example, reducing the use of diapers, especially disposables, also reduces the chances of urinary tract infections. "Babies are especially vulnerable to urinary tract infections, or UTIs, because the stool in their diapers can introduce bacteria into the urethra, the tube that carries urine from the bladder. Girls get UTIs more often than boys do because their urethra is short and straight, providing an easy path for bacteria to invade the bladder, the ureters, and—in rare, more serious cases—the kidneys."[21]

Doctors, pediatricians and nurses who visit countries where infant pottying is the norm typically have a favorable opinion of the method if they take the time to meet, observe and speak with practitioners. Curious or skeptical visitors to these areas will be told politely and in no uncertain terms that babies are satisfactorily toilet trained between the ages of 6 and 15 months. Parents will smile or laugh if you try to convince them otherwise.

Some physicians who travel abroad observe families using this method but are convinced that it can only work in foreign cultures and settings. This implies that Westerners are not capable of working closely with their babies and do not want to spend the necessary time with their babies. They are mistaken about this in that there are indeed Western families who want to devote the needed time.

Chapter 8
Environment & Diapers

Perhaps not a day passes without some scary gloom-and-doom environmental statistics being paraded in front of us or forced down our heavily polluted throats. Everything, it seems, is bad for us, bad for our health, bad for the world, bad for the atmosphere and bad for . . . baby!

While the selection of a preferred toilet teaching technique is certainly not a life-and-death issue, there are consequences beyond convenience to consider. Many concerned families are first attracted to infant pottying when they learn how environmentally sound and beneficial it is. The important thing to remember here is that "you can make a difference."

An average baby uses 6,000–8,000 diapers by the time conventional toilet training is completed—and the quantity is increasing among families who delay longer and longer. It is not uncommon to use up to 10,000 diapers per child. Whichever type of diaper is used, tremendous amounts of resources are required to manufacture and clean or dispose of them.

Although it may be more convenient in some respects to use traditional diapering methods for two to four years, the detrimental effects of "full-time diapers" (whether disposable or cloth) on the environment cannot be denied. By reducing or eliminating the use of diapers, you personally can conserve natural resources and reduce pollution.

Water

Tremendous amounts of water are heated and used to clean the following:

- cloth diapers
- dirty baby bottoms, hands, legs and other body parts
- wet/soiled baby clothes, bedding, towels, mattress covers
- caregiver's hands after changing diapers

Water is polluted by laundering cloth diapers and manufacturing disposable diapers. Flushing disposable diapers down the toilet clogs sewer lines, creates tons of extra sludge each year and wastes large amounts of water.[22]

Trees

More than one billion trees go into the manufacture of disposable diapers in one year.[23] It takes the pulp from one tree to make 500 to 1,000 disposable diapers.[24] At that rate, you save 10 to 20 trees per child by using the infant potty technique.[25]

Manufacturers of disposable diapers claim that the tree population is actually increasing thanks to them. The fact that tree farming is profitable encourages the planting and careful management of more and more trees as the demand increases. This, they say, results in more trees being planted than are cut down. No rare or endangered trees are used to make disposable diapers.[26]

Landfills

Nobody thinks twice about making a mountain out of a landfill. And this is what appears to be happening all over the Western world, and in particular, the USA. Although the statistics vary and there is no way to determine exact figures, it must be evident even to the most environmentally disinterested that disposable diapers take a lot of space in landfills. Diapers are the third most dumped consumer product found in American landfills (after fast food containers and newspapers).[27] The number of disposable diapers used in a year in the USA is staggering, somewhere around 20 billion.[28] This translates to more than five million tons buried in landfills each year. The annual cost to taxpayers for disposal of disposable diapers is now near half a billion dollars.

Groundwater can become contaminated by viruses carried in the human feces and urine from disposable diapers. Flies and other insects drawn to the diapers can also spread viruses and bacteria. The most common diseases that are currently spread via diaper waste in landfills in Western countries are:

- enteroviruses (diarrhea and other intestinal diseases)
- rhinoviruses (influenza, common cold, etc.)[29]

In lesser developed lands, the situation becomes more hazardous to the health. More than 100 different intestinal viruses can be excreted in human feces, including hepatitis and—via vaccines passed in urine—polio. Although disposable diapers are used in far greater quantities in Western compared to third world countries, use of disposables is gradually increasing in the larger cities of many nonindustrialized societies. Finally, traces of the toxic industrial contaminant dioxin can be found in disposable diapers. This can be harmful to both baby and the environment.

Biodegradable?

So-called biodegradable diapers are made of cornstarch-based plastic, biodegradable elastic, wood pulp and rayon, and they are chemical free. However, biodegradable disposable diapers don't solve the landfill problem. They have been shown to decompose in two to five years in a laboratory, but in fact take much longer (up to 500 years) to decompose in a landfill, due to compaction and lack of sunlight, water and oxygen.[30] Although they may decompose faster than standard disposable diapers, they still use the same space in landfills, and the health risks are the same. The only way for biodegradable diapers to be environmentally effective is to have them processed by a sewage treatment plant.

Diaper Services

Diaper services are not a very environmentally friendly solution to pollution. In some ways, use of a diaper service merely passes the problems on to someone else.

Many of the services use large amounts of toxic chemicals, including chlorine bleach and other polluting agents, to get the diapers as white as possible. The diapers must be collected and delivered, requiring fuel and adding to traffic congestion and air pollution.

For parents who prefer to use a diaper service, here are some positive points to ponder. Less electrical energy is used this way since the diapers are washed collectively.[31] Cloth diapers can be reused, and this spares trees. Plastics and other unnatural materials are not present in cotton diapers. Using a diaper service is cheaper than buying disposable diapers. You don't need to make frequent trips to the shop to buy disposables since you only need a fixed supply of cloth diapers. You will reduce your weekly garbage pile and cut down on waste going into landfills. Last but not least, you can send the laundry out for someone else to do.

So What?

Despite the statistics cited in this chapter and the fact that a widespread educational campaign could greatly benefit the environment, environmental groups have, for all intents and purposes, remained indifferent to the idea of reducing or eliminating diapers through infant pottying. The most any organization has done so far is to publish a brief review about the infant potty technique. IPT is not an easy sell. There are no frightening or heart-rending photos that can be used to outrage the population in order to extract large donations or allow the media to sensationalize the topic.

Another disinterested group consists of parenting magazines, even those advocating a natural lifestyle. Both mainstream and alternative parenting magazines find infant pottying too inconvenient to even mention to their readers. In addition, magazines lack the courage to write about it, preferring to remain loyal to lucrative advertising "diaper dollars."

On an individual level, parents may think, "So what? Who cares about these environmental statistics?" One baby's worth of diapers may not seem to matter. But when the diapers of hundreds or thousands of babies are compiled, compacted or cleansed, the toll on the environment and our natural resources is staggering. It is our children and grandchildren who will have to deal with the mess we are making. We, as responsible adults, should cut back on pollution and depletion whenever and wherever reasonably possible. One effective way to do so is to reduce or eliminate the use of diapers by starting toilet teaching in infancy or as soon as you first hear about it. Since environmental groups have so far not embraced the cause and the media and parenting magazines don't dare broach the topic, the role of individual responsibility takes on tremendous importance here.

Minimal Use of Diapers

Part-time use of diapers is one of the ways infant pottying has been adapted to Western culture. Until relatively recently in human history, diapers or diaper substitutes have played almost no role in child rearing. While the majority of parents in rural Asian and African villages do not use any diapers at all, most IPT parents in Western countries prefer to use diapers on infants on occasions where wetting or soiling can be troublesome, such as on trips or outings, when baby is ill, at night if baby wets the bed on a regular basis or between potty sessions while baby is physically too small to wear training pants.

Infant potty parents drastically reduce the number of diapers used compared to what is required for full-time diapering. Most prefer cloth diapers to disposables. They prefer keeping baby in cotton and other natural fibers. They tend to be more vigilant at pottying and changing, and find that infants wearing cloth are more aware of elimination too. Some have found that their babies willingly pee in disposable diapers at night but not in underwear or cotton "dipes." IPT parents are likely to stay at home with baby or arrange one-on-one care in order to have someone reliable available to potty baby—or expeditiously change dirty diapers—and thus do not feel a need for the conveniences of disposable diapers. They also tend to believe that using cloth diapers is better for the environment than using disposables.

It is important to note that the infant potty approach does not in any way exclude the use of disposable diapers for parents who prefer them. Both types of diaper are compatible with the method. The "bottom line" is to reduce and then eliminate the use of diapers as soon as possible. Another advantage is that IPT families can save a considerable amount of money on diapers, laundry, water and other costs, on average $1,500–$2,500 per child.

Infant potty families should not be too hard on themselves. Although the ideal situation would be to eliminate diapers altogether from birth, this is not practical or realistic for most. It is important to find a balance between infant elimination training and other activities. Don't be so fanatic about it that you lose your perspective. It is better for your baby to pee in a diaper on occasion than to be around an uptight or exhausted parent obsessing about "potty perfection."

Cloth or Disposable Diapers?

There are convincing arguments on both sides of the cloth-versus-disposable-diaper debate. Manufacturers and marketers present compelling cases for the superiority of their respective products and the inferiority of their competitors' diapers. Parents need to consider and weigh the facts in relation to their own particular circumstances and lifestyle, then make an informed decision. There are situations where parents may prefer to use one type of diaper but are forced to use another. Don't worry or feel guilty about not being able to use a particular type of diaper if it jeopardizes the health or well-being of your baby.

Some of the main factors to consider when choosing diapers are cost, health, convenience and environment.

Pro-Cloth & Anti-Disposable Arguments

- Cotton is natural and soft and lets baby's skin breathe.
- Cotton diapers are far cheaper to purchase than disposable diapers since only a few dozen cloth diapers are needed as opposed to thousands of disposables. Your savings increase if the cloth diapers are re-used with any future children you may have.
- With cloth diapers, you avoid chemical gels, dyes and other possible synthetic irritants. The super-absorbent polyacrylate (SAP) in disposables absorbs urine and stores it as a gel next to baby's skin. For sensitive babies, this chemical can be toxic. It can also stick to infants' genitals. Some of the other ingredients of disposables are heavily treated pulp/cellulose, polyethylene, glues, dyes and synthetic perfumes. The toxic chemical dioxin may also be present in them.[32]
- Good diapering practices (changing and laundering) can make cloth the equal of disposables in terms of staying dry and avoiding diaper rash.
- Parents don't need to make frequent trips to the store since they only need a fixed supply of cloth diapers.

- Diaper liners catch stools so you don't have to rinse the entire diaper after each poop.
- The word "disposable" leads parents to believe they can dispose of dirty diapers without any effort or bother, yet baby's skin usually needs cleaning with each change of a diaper, and it takes hundreds of years for disposables to decompose in landfills.
- The chemical dryness of disposables lets parents delay changing diapers under the false pretense, "As long as it feels dry, it's all right for baby."[33]
- The feeling of dryness of disposables delays the learning of cause and effect and can add months or as much as one to two years to toilet training a baby who wears diapers full time.
- A cotton diaper has a multitude of handy and baby-friendly uses, including serving as a washcloth, towel, light cover, cushion, sunshade, bib and toy (peekaboo).

Pro-Disposable & Anti-Cloth Arguments

- Child-care centers usually require disposables.
- Disposables are more convenient since you can just throw them away and forget about them.
- Using disposables drastically reduces laundry.
- Disposables are adapted to fast-paced living where parents feel "time challenged" due to work or other reasons.
- Baby feels dry due to the absorption of moisture by disposables.
- For some, disposables may be healthier for the skin and reduce or eliminate diaper rash since they keep baby dry.
- Bad smells are less offensive than with cloth diapers.
- Parents can get away with being lazy about changing diapers.
- Babies and parents are less likely to awake in the middle of the night if baby pees in an absorbent disposable diaper.
- With a severe rash such as one caused by a yeast infection, disposables may be the only way to ensure baby stays rash free. Since yeast is resistant to hot water and detergent, cloth diapers can continually reinfect baby.

Diaper Rash

The term "diaper rash" refers to a variety of rashes that occur in the area of the body covered by a diaper. Genetics and hygiene contribute to the occurrence or lack of diaper rash. The different types of rash have different causes, but all are exacerbated by wet skin. Causes include:

- friction (typically where moist inner thighs rub together or where elastic rubs the wet skin)
- skin bacteria (bacteria begin to form as soon as baby wets or soils a diaper or other underwear)
- irritated skin (typically resulting from skin contact with soaps, detergents or lotions)
- allergic reaction (can affect more than just the diapered area)
- psoriasis (a skin disease that affects more than just the diapered area)
- yeast infections

Most parents have found that diaper rash can be relieved by letting baby be bare-bottomed at times. Exposing skin to air is a natural and gentle way to let it dry and be free of irritants.[34]

Diaper rash can be a blessing in disguise if it leads parents to try infant potty-ing and gives baby the gift of early emancipation from diapers. Families practicing the infant potty technique on a fairly regular and consistent basis rarely encounter diaper rash since their babies are rarely in wet or soiled garments.

Diaper Bulk Blues

Imagine an infant, developmentally ready to turn over for the first time ever, being denied this joy for days or weeks whenever she is wrapped in diaper bulk. Or being deprived of the freedom to simply grab her toes whenever she wants, except during diaper changes. Babies love to do all sorts of things with their feet and will touch, grab, hold, gaze at and play with them constantly, often pulling them in front of their face, if given the chance. This early natural behavior must have a purpose, yet is limited by diaper wearing. How about the joys of wiggling and squirming naked or in a T-shirt, being able to twist and bend as far as your little body, joints and muscles will allow, without restriction. Or feeling, exploring and being touched on that whole sensitive area of your body, from waist to thighs, that is otherwise often "out of bounds."

More sophisticated coordination can be hampered too. Parents who let their babies go diaperless during some or all of the day report that their children scoot, sit, crawl, squat and walk sooner than when swaddled in diapers. By reducing dia-per use, you are not only advancing infant toileting and helping the environment. You are also giving your baby a head start in physical development.

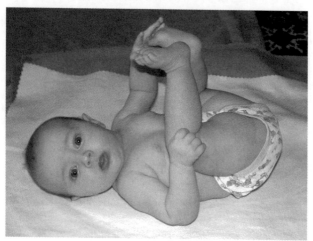

Friederike Bradfisch

4-month-old Jutta, unrestricted by diaper bulk and free to explore her feet.

Chapter 9
The Myths

This chapter presents a compilation of counterarguments to classic challenges made by disbelievers. Everyone has an opinion about potty training, and these opinions will likely disagree with yours. Friends, relatives and sometimes even strangers will offer advice, much of it unwanted. If they are not familiar with infant pottying, they will probably find it strange.

Skepticism from family members, friends and neighbors can be tough to handle. It is nice to discover that you are not alone! There is a growing online community of enthusiastic mothers who will gladly offer you inspiration and share their wisdom and experiences. You can also join or start a local play and support group. You may be able to find support and encouragement from relatives who are familiar with infant toileting. It is surprising how many immigrants and grandparents are acquainted with the method. It is like a breath of fresh air to speak with those who can tell you about their own experiences. But for now, if you are facing negativity and resistance, you may find it helpful to read and reflect on ways myths and rumors can be dispelled.

"It's about Potty-Trained Parents" . . .

This argument implies that baby has nothing to do with the infant potty technique. The fact is, an infant has some control over urination and defecation, and this ability improves gradually over the months with the help of an attentive caregiver, until total control is achieved.

Does the fact that a baby cannot feed himself mean we should not feed him? Does the fact that a baby cannot dress himself mean we should not keep him in clean clothing? Does the fact that a baby cannot change a diaper mean we should let him be soiled and wet? The answer to these and similar questions is, of course, no. Then why should a willing parent be criticized for using and responding to elimination communication and for taking care of baby's toilet needs in a loving and different way at a relatively young age?

Newborns and infants cannot be viewed as independent of their caregivers since without them they would not survive. The fact that infant pottying is not necessary for survival does not mean it is without merit.

"It's Purely a Matter of Catching" . . .

Some may argue that infant pottying is basically about "catching" baby's pee or poo at the right time and that this is merely a matter of luck. This is indeed part of the equation, especially at the start, but certainly not the whole equation. If you start early enough, baby will be and remain aware of this bodily function. For the first few days or weeks as you are learning to communicate with each other about elimination, it might well be a question of "catching" his waste in a receptacle, but once you are familiar with his timing, body language and signals, and once he associates your cues with the function of elimination, it becomes a question of "being there on time" for baby.

"It's too Inconvenient" . . .

Some Americans lapse into a fast-food mentality when it comes to raising children—and especially when it comes to potty training. They want it fast, they want it now and they want it to be easy; otherwise, they opt to put it off for as long as they can. Now that disposable diapers are more absorbent than ever and, through the use of super absorbent gels, give babies the feeling of being dry the moment they pee, Americans are delaying potty training even longer. Daycare centers abound with children ages 3 and 4 who have not yet begun, and disposables have increased the largest size to size six.

Each time baby poos, and frequently when he pees, something must be done. Parents can do that "something" immediately before the fact or else sometime after the fact. Either way, elimination requires attention, time and energy. It is a matter of preference how a parent decides to take care of the situation.

When Westerners first hear of infant pottying, their reaction is one of disbelief and disapproval. "That's just too inconvenient!" is a common defense. Fortunately, not everyone likes or agrees with the concepts of having babies for convenience and "convenience comes first." Don't let those who elect to delay toilet teaching convince you to delay too.

"It's for Parents' Convenience" . . .

Some believe that helping baby avoid wetting or soiling a diaper is a matter of convenience for caregivers and is "Victorian and repressive." Readers of this book will note that not one of the testimonials refers to the infant potty technique as a "convenient" method and that this claim is not made anywhere in the book. It has been repeatedly emphasized that it takes dedicated, devoted, patient and diligent caregivers to work closely with baby. Granted, mothers appreciate not having to clean diapers, but this is also beneficial for baby since it is far more hygienic and comfortable not to sit in a soiled diaper. In addition, many babies dislike being held down for diaper changes, and the battles resulting from this increase over time.

The word "repressive" refers to excluding something from the conscious mind. This book repeatedly refers to the stimulation and encouragement of baby's awareness of elimination functions, as well as to the symbiotic relationship of mutual benefit to baby and caregiver that develops. Indispensable elements of this close relationship include bonding, intimacy, communication, caring, patience and respect.

"Baby Isn't Ready" . . .

Baby is ready! Western medicine teaches that children are not physically or psychologically ready to start toilet training until they are 18 months or older (Europe) or 2–3 years old (United States). Both have been disproved by billions of families around the world. In other societies, parental communication, expectations, training and guidance are the keys to readiness and success.

One could make the argument that infants aren't ready for conventional toilet training, and this is true in the sense that an infant can't say "pee" or "poo," cannot walk to the potty or sit down on his own, etc. But these prerequisites are irrelevant where infants are concerned. As one mother put it, "It's like saying a baby is not ready to learn to walk before he can tie his shoes."

"It's Dangerous" . . .

Those who declare that infant toileting is harmful have never met or carefully observed a family using it and have no idea what it entails. Instead, they read accounts that refer to a different method of early toilet training. Furthermore, children's psychological problems, if any, usually stem from their overall relationship or a lack of communication with their parents rather than from one particular aspect or phase.

"It's Impossible" . . .

Upon first hearing about IPT, many assume it's fake or just a passing fad. The denial is so strong that some refuse to believe toilet training accounts coming from their own mothers. A defeatist attitude guarantees failure. In other societies, families know it is possible. The combination of their history and confident attitude go a long way towards making it possible.

"It Takes Just as Long" . . .

A favorite argument used to discourage families from adopting infant potty teamwork is to claim that toilet training takes equally as long, or even longer, when you start in infancy. This is generally false if infant pottying is done correctly, especially if the years of diapers and diapering of conventional training are included in the equation. But even more important, infant pottying is not about competition or finishing at a certain age.

"Wearing Diapers Is Part of Being a Baby" . . .

Some parents feel that wearing diapers is part of being a baby and that infant toileting is a way to "rush baby to grow up." They want baby to be a baby as long as possible, and this includes using diapers. This is a matter of preference and choice.

There have been, and still are, far more babies in the world raised without diapers than with diapers. Babies are born with the ability to communicate about elimination. The fact that some parents choose to recognize and respond to a baby's elimination communication does not mean their baby is being forced to grow up in a hurry. Any tool that enhances communication between baby and caregiver is valuable. A baby who pees in a receptacle is just as much a baby as a baby who pees in a diaper.

"It's Unhygienic" . . .

The idea of babies going diaperless leads some to conclude that these babies pee and poo all over the house. While some diaperless babies have occasional accidents indoors, infant pottying does not involve letting children eliminate whenever and wherever they please.

"It's Obsessing about Bowel Movements" . . .

This is another ridiculous argument that has nothing to do with reality. Again, it is offered out of ignorance, by those who are referring to a different method of toilet training infants or to their own strange hang-ups. There is no obsessing about bowel movements. Instead, caregivers are attentive and watch for signals from baby, in order to know when to take baby to go. There is certainly nothing wrong or obsessive with monitoring and being receptive to baby's signals and natural timing.

"Freud Says" . . .

Sigmund Freud's famous but outdated postulation that early toilet training leads to the development of the anal character traits of orderliness, cleanliness and miserliness has never been proven. The theory is good fodder for gossip but nothing more. The influence of toilet training on personality is debatable at best, with many psychologists believing that Freud's list of character traits are the by-product of other child-rearing practices or the child's upbringing as a whole. In any case, his theory was based on a different and harsh method of early toilet training, one which is not advocated in this book.

Chapter 10
Testimonials

A selection of four testimonials is included here. These have been shortened from their original length in my much expanded book *Infant Potty Training*. Additional detailed testimonials—not only from the USA but from many other countries—can also be found in that book.

A Physician Speaks Out

Dr. Lauri Nandyal graduated from medical school in Cincinnati in 1989 and completed her family practice residency in 1992. She worked in rural Ohio for four years until 1996, doing full-scope family practice including obstetrics and, consequently, a lot of pediatrics. Lauri has three girls of her own, ages 8 years, 5 years and 1 year old. Since her third child was born, she has reduced her clinical work in order to stay home with her family. Here is what the doctor had to report in 2000.

I didn't learn about this method of toilet training in time to use with my first two girls. As a physician, I had never even given this type of thing a moment's consideration. Even in my many travels before motherhood, I was oblivious to the practice of infant toileting. It's just one of those things that doesn't enter your consciousness until you're a parent. Plus, in medical school we're taught that it's physically impossible to toilet train an infant, and this is what we tell our patients. So the concept really took me by surprise.

My neighbor from India told me how she had toilet trained her children. Her method involved holding her baby on her feet. After a feeding, she would sit on the floor or the bed and prop her baby on her feet over a newspaper or a diaper, and in response, he would "perform." She further mentioned that in India, at least in more traditional families, mothers carry or hold their babies much of the time, and babies don't wear diapers. One way mothers stay dry is to take their babies to the toilet every 45–60 minutes and prompt them to go. They may squat the babies in a corner in the bathroom or outside and make a "sssss" noise to cue them to go.

Aside from the initial explanation by my neighbor, my learning process consisted mainly of on-the-job training. I didn't find any books about this until my baby was about 9 months old. At that time, I read a chapter in a book on toilet training which mentioned "other methods" and gave some credence to early toilet training but did not really encourage it. That was the extent of the literature I found until Laurie Boucke's *Trickle Treat*.

Since I really didn't feel comfortable with the actual method my neighbor described and since I figured that the procedure would eventually lead to using a toilet anyway, I decided to start there—that is, using the toilet—from the beginning. The position I use with my daughter involves me squatting in front of the toilet or else sitting on a small stool placed at the front of it. I prop my elbows on my knees and hold her securely with a hand under each armpit. In this way I was able to support her head until she had good head control. She is in a squatting position over the toilet, facing me, with her bottom hanging over the toilet bowl. One word of warning: Little girls can "shoot" when they urinate. If my baby is not aimed downward, she'll pee on me and the toilet seat. I have to lean her a little forward to pee straight down. If she doesn't really need to go, she may resist me positioning her. I've come to trust her knowing when she's done too. She'll straighten out her legs and stand upright. Occasionally, I've hurried her off before this signal, only to be sorry later. We use diapers between potty sessions, mainly because I can't find any training pants that are small enough to fit her. (The smallest are size two. I guess they figure no one here buys size one, but they must be selling them somewhere!) When she goes in the toilet, I usually say "good girl" or give her a kiss. I don't jump up and down with excitement. I did at first because I was so surprised, but now I'm a bit more matter of fact, just smile and say "good job" or something like that. At night we use a diaper, to spare the bed from accidents.

I started by concentrating on bowel movements rather than urination. I waited a while after a feeding, anywhere from 10 to 30 minutes, then held her over the toilet. I was amazed the first time it worked. We eventually got her BM routine down really well. Since about 6 weeks of age, she has rarely soiled a diaper even while awake.

As for our prompting the baby to go, we grunt or make a bearing-down noise to cue bowel movements. We also have been trying some baby sign language. We may hold, pinch or wrinkle our nose, as a sort of "stinky" or smelly sign, to ask her if she has to go. For urinating, we make a water-flowing sound.

When our daughter was 9 months old, we spent 3 weeks in India. My husband is from Andhra Pradesh, India. While there, I interviewed my sisters-in-law about infant toilet training. My husband was unaware of how he had been toilet trained in infancy. He was the last of 10 children and since this isn't something that most fathers do with their babies anyway, he was not familiar with this method.

Sure, this method seems inconvenient. Some days I dedicate an hour to the potty if you add it all up. It's just another thing to think about, and our society is too busy, too distracted with so many things to do. My reasoning is that we have to deal with our babies' bottoms one way or another, and we can do it right from the beginning or postpone the process and have to reeducate the child later when it may be a bigger hassle. We can't change this pattern unless we really have the will to change. It's a mother's individual decision. I don't feel badly if someone honestly admits she is too busy to do this. I think, though, if more people really understood the impact on the environment and the potential harm it can do to children sitting around in wet diapers or by exposing children to chemicals like dioxin for so long, parents might be more motivated to try this. As a physician, if I see a mother whose baby has diaper rash, I'm able to prod her a little and recommend the child be in cloth or "flapping in the breeze" or that something "new and different" be done like infant pottying. There has to be a motivation to change behavior. Our society doesn't make it easy. Paper diapers are just too darn convenient . . . at quite a price.

I pooh-pooh the stories about psychological damage resulting from infant toileting. I have read the comments of Freudian psychologists and think the concern about trauma has only to do with the coercive way early toilet training was practiced in the early 1900s. Back then, folks were encouraged to tie their kids to potty chairs and got angry at them if they didn't perform. Of course, that was a warped approach. Spending time with your child and playing with her cannot be harmful even if it's on a potty. Obviously, I never leave my baby alone on the potty at this age. If my daughter is tired of sitting on the toilet, I quit. I never force it on her. My baby enjoys spending time with me wherever we are. I strongly feel that this method cannot harm my baby any more, and likely much less, than the customary Western way that I used with my older two whom I began retraining around the age of 2 years.

Western medicine teaches that it is not possible neurologically for babies to be toilet trained in infancy. I don't know where that idea came from. It appears to be "medlore," simply something that somebody passed on from their own experience. It's not coming from an in-depth study on the topic that I've ever found. What the layperson doesn't realize is how much of medicine is just hearsay. We don't have "randomized, double-blind, placebo-controlled" studies backing up more than about 30% of what we do. Much of medicine is an art or approach that has been passed along. Our present advice on postponing toilet training until 15 months or later due to "neurologic immaturity" is obviously ignorant, given the wealth of evidence to the contrary in cross-cultural reports. Who should you believe, millions of babies dry by age 6–9 months or the so-called experts?

The medical community may play a word game with you and say that an infant isn't consciously continent, or isn't holding it, but just letting go in a timely fashion or due to conditioned reflexes. You can rename it whatever you want, but the fact is, my child can stay dry longer than it takes for her bladder to fill up. She can hold it. There is no question, if you wait until 1 or 1 ½ years to start introducing babies to the toilet, it will take them a while to unlearn what you taught them and accept the new rules. But if they start with a continence program at birth, they will know that there is more to life than just sitting in a diaper. Although my personal experience with infant toilet training is limited to one child, I know that the rest of the world doesn't toilet train the Western way. My sisters-in-law have children who stayed dry day and night at the age of 6 months, so I know our babies have more control than we think they do.

Another factor in suppressing this technique of infant toileting education in the United States is commercialism. Too often, doctors are unwittingly fronts for a particular marketeer—whether it be a pharmaceutical, baby formula or diaper company. I am very aware of how much of my education about prescription drugs came from pharmaceutical representatives who had a product to sell. Manufacturers of disposable diapers have everything to lose from doctors encouraging the infant toileting method or the use of cloth diapers. From the start, hospitals provide paper diapers, which they say are more sanitary than cloth diapers, but all doctors know it is the caregiver's hands that are the real culprits in the spread of germs and that the type of diaper has little to do with it. It's very difficult to get into the ivory towers of medicine. It is a real challenge to change the way doctors get their information. Now that about one third of doctors in the USA are women and many of them are mothers, these issues may be more open to dialogue and reeducation.

I think Western medicine will slowly accept the principles of infant toilet training. Minds are opening because patients are demanding more alternative approaches. Given a little more time and publicity about this issue, I think it will become more welcome in the West. It's a slow process until we "die off" some of the older ways of doing things. I hope we don't have to wait until we suffer more consequences from the environmental impact of our "conveniences." As cultures rub against other cultures and patients begin to pressure their doctors for new information, doctors will become more receptive. It's a revolution that needs to happen.

Elimination Communication – An Intuitive Approach

Rosie Wilde lives in Seattle. She discovered infant pottying when her first son Dakota was 3 months old. Dakota finished at 22 months. Rosie started at birth with her second son Ian, who was 14 months old at the time this interview was updated in 2002. Rosie has a web site dedicated to the topic of what she calls elimination communication ("ec") and has introduced many families to this method via her website, hard work and enthusiasm.

First Son . . .

My first son was 3 months old when I stumbled upon this method. I was surfing around on the Internet and found an article on elimination training in infancy. I read part of it but was so upset by it that I turned off the computer. My upset was due to skepticism about being able to do this within the confines of our culture. My curiosity got the better of me, and I switched the computer back on and continued reading. Before reaching the end of the article, I stood up, went to Dakota's changing table, took his diaper off and said, "We're going to try something different. If you need to pee or poop, try and let me know. I'll try to understand you. If I don't seem to get it, try telling me another way. We're both going to make mistakes. We'll do this for one hour and see how it feels." I returned to the computer to read the rest of the article. Before I had finished, he wiggled, squirmed and grunted a bit. I took him to the bathroom, and he pooped for me. We continued doing it from that first day until he was finished with toilet training at 22 months.

For about the first month, I carried him around with a flannel under his bottom, until I learned his signals. Up to 4 months of age, I kept a little bucket in the room with us, but then he started letting me know far enough in advance that I could take him to the bathroom. He preferred going in the bathroom where he saw us use the toilet and soon refused to use the bucket anymore.

We had varying degrees of success over the months, depending on his mood. He was a pretty high-needs child. At times he was involved in teething or learning a skill and didn't pay attention. There were a few difficult days where we missed nearly every pee or poop. No matter what happened, it was always a cooperative effort between us, and I learned not to fear making mistakes. Some days we "hit the pot" 90% of the time; on other days just 75%. Either way, we were connecting all the time, and I loved it.

With my son, the communication was often by psychic means. This meant I had to be tuned in to him. It might sound strange, but I often heard the word "pee" in my mind when he had to pee or poop. It was very clear. Whenever I received that communication, I took him to the bathroom and he'd go. I don't communicate telepathically in other ways, so it was very hard for me to trust it.

My husband had the same experience with hearing "pee" in his mind. When Dakota got older, a very good friend of mine named Alice started coparenting with us, and she had the same experience too. She would suddenly hear the word "pee" in her head, take him to pee and he'd go for her. For people who wonder whether or not babies are telepathic, we have anecdotal evidence that they are!

The communication with my son was not only psychic in terms of hearing a word, but I eventually realized that I was also feeling it in my body. Dakota signaled me in a number of other ways. I had the best results reading his signals when he was in the sling and when I was relaxed about the whole thing. I made the "pss pss" noise in an attempt to get him to vocally signal to me ahead of time. He started making this noise around 7 months, but only when we were out in public. He would also holler ("Mama, Mama!"), cry (usually only when waking up with a full bladder), crawl to the bathroom door or crawl to me and look at me. The times I missed getting him to the bathroom were when I was not focused—talking to someone, reading or otherwise not tuned in to Dakota.

When he started scooting and crawling, things got a little confusing. He peed on the floor a lot without giving any cues. We figured out that the pressure on his tummy and bladder made it difficult to control his bladder. We placed him on a mat during this phase. In the same vein, sometimes he would be playing on his belly, ask to pee but when we got to the bathroom, nothing happened. I think that when we picked him up, the pressure on his belly was reduced, and he no longer felt the urge to pee.

In general, the only time I diapered him was to take him shopping. I always asked him to let me know if he had to pee and assured him that I'd take him to a nearby place, remove the diaper and let him go. When we got home half an hour later, his diaper would be dry. This was a baby who normally peed every 10 minutes. This told me right away that he had an ability to hold it if he wanted, at least up to a certain point.

By the age of 7 months, he had reasonable control. We didn't have to diaper him anymore to take him on a 30-minute trip to the grocery store. By 9½ months, he always told me if he had to go, unless he was teething, preoccupied or in a resistant phase of saying no to everything. At 11 months, he only peed about once an hour, and if we were outside or driving in the car, he was great about signaling me verbally. By 14 months, he took care of all his own pooping. Of course, I had to wipe his bottom, but he walked to the potty and sat down on his own. Sometimes he said "poop" to call me to come and sit next to him.

Around the age of 11 months, Dakota went through a really intense potty strike for 6 weeks. He stopped signaling, and when we took him to the sink to pee, he arched his back and yelled. During that time, we diapered him. That was the only time he wore diapers throughout the day. He didn't like it at all. He preferred going bare-bottomed or wearing pants because they were less restrictive than a cloth diaper. I finally found the cause of his strike. He wanted to use the big toilet instead of a potty. Once I figured it out, he started signaling again.

Second Son . . .

I started at birth with my second son Ian. I'm much more relaxed this time. It's the same with other things you experience with your first and second child. You are more relaxed with everything, like nursing or when they fall down.

It felt like a cooperative arrangement with Ian right from the beginning. I felt like, "We are doing this together, and if we have off days, we're having off days together." I'd have days where I just couldn't deal with it and I'd tell him, and we'd take a break.

If Ian is teething and peeing on me, I just think, "Oh, you're teething." When he was smaller, I'd just put a flannel under him and knew we'd be back to it again the next day. It was the same when he went through his learning-to-crawl phase. It took him a long time to learn to crawl. It took about 2 months, and during that time, his message was, "Do not bug me about elimination communication!" And it didn't bother me. "Okay, fine. I know we'll just pick this up again in a month." And right now, he's learning to walk and we're doing the same thing again.

People often say, "It's your second baby. You must not have any messes now since you're so good at it." I tell them that, on the contrary, because I'm not sitting around stressing over it and because I've made up my mind that if we were living in an indigenous environment with dirt floors, babies on the floor wouldn't have any need to signal—and that's why they don't like to signal when they are on the floor or learning how to walk—I just don't worry about the times he pees when he's down crawling or learning to walk. I pay a lot of attention to him when he's in-arms or we're in bed, and I trust that in the next few months, he'll start coming to me more and more when he's on the floor.

With Ian, I don't hear the word "pee" in my mind when he needs to go. I just have a sense that "it's time for Ian to go."

I found this method very easy, far superior to any of the alternatives. It was easier than the mechanical work of diapering and washing diapers. I much pre-ferred spending time focusing on my sons and reading their cues to dealing with diapers and laundry. In addition, it was good for the environment, cost free and perfectly compatible with our lifestyle. It promoted all the positive aspects of at-tached child rearing that I wanted to include. It went along with breastfeeding, meeting my children's needs, carrying them in a sling and not leaving them alone with another caregiver in infancy.

On my web site, I advocate elimination communication as part of evolutionary behavior. I've had mostly positive feedback on the site, but one lady was upset at this idea. I think it is because if you believe in evolution, you have to work hard to justify not using this method.

To visit Rosie's website and e-mail list:
www.committed.to/ec or www.babieswithoutdiapers.com

A 10-Month-Old Graduate

Lois Baas is a nurse living in Holland, Michigan. She has a BSN from Calvin College. Her husband, Craig, has a BA in psychology. Lois gave up her nursing career to be a stay-at-home mom. She made a conscious decision to use cloth diapers instead of disposables, unaware that there was an even better option to consider, until she read a short piece about "potty untraining." It had very little "how-to" advice but enough information to inspire her to give it a try. Her son responded impressively to the devo-tion of, and close communication with, both of his parents and their attentiveness to his elimination needs. Much to their surprise and delight, Zachary graduated at 10 months of age. At this point, he met the criteria identified by the Asian and African definition of "toilet trained," namely, being basically accident-free combined with good communication skills that allowed him to signal his toilet needs to his parents. Their amazing story, submitted in 2002 when their son was 2½ years old, follows. Bear in mind that finishing this young in the West is exceptional, and you should **not** *expect the same results. Please do not feel discouraged if your baby takes considerably longer.*

From his birth, I had our son wearing cloth diapers with vinyl covers during the day and a disposable for nights. When I began this method, I did away with the vinyl cover when at home during the day and began using cloth diapers with a vinyl cover at night. This way I could easily identify when he peed, as the cloth diaper was obviously wet. I replaced the diaper in between toilet visits and changed it diligently when any sign of wetness occurred during the day.

The first time I tried to pee Zachary, he went! This was very encouraging and gave me the incentive to continue to pursue this approach. Zachary already had good back and neck control, and I positioned him on the adult toilet, supporting him against myself as I straddled the seat, sitting (or standing at times) behind him as we faced away from the tank. I was not about to get peed on if possible! As he went, I would say "pee pee," and it wasn't long before positioning him and giving him this verbal cue was all he needed. Eventually all I had to do was position him and he knew to eliminate.

Bowel movements were easy to identify as Zachary's cues were obvious. He would grunt and grimace, and his face would flush. Observing this, I would take him to the toilet and position him as I did with peeing, and as he went, I would give the cue "do do." At home, positioning in response to these overt cues was eventually all that was necessary. On a rare occasion, if he needed redirection or was away from home, the verbal cue came in handy. At 10 months, he was signing and giving other cues (mentioned later) for the potty.

"Catching" pees was elusive for a while. It seemed to be a hit-or-miss phenomenon as Zachary didn't have any obvious cues with these for some time. As I look back, I believe I was gradually tuning in to some sort of timing while I also became aware of his anatomical cues of slight scrotum contraction and penis extension—especially with an impending pee. If I missed a pee or noticed Zachary in the process, I would give the verbal cue "pee pee," remove his diaper and position him on the toilet to reinforce where to "go." As he gained even more control, he would stop and wait for me to sit him on the toilet before finishing. Initially, running a stream of warm water from a peri-bottle (squeeze bottle) between his legs and/or running the tap would often promote an impending pee, helping him to relax when first learning. Sometimes other types of distraction helped, like a quick visit from his pet dalmatian or Daddy. Often just sitting for a short time was all it took, with Zachary looking up adoringly at me and my returning his gaze with smiles.

I believe he learned to associate his body's response to relaxing to my verbal cue of "relax" as we implemented the above. This wasn't intentional training, but did prove beneficial to the ongoing process. If Zachary ever became fussy or signaled to get off the toilet by arching or stiffening up, I would take him off and leave the bathroom, keeping him in-arms and diaperless. I figured those times he didn't have to go yet, but with his great frequency, I anticipated he would need to go soon and would return within 5–10 minutes to try again, with success. Doing this probably helped me discover his timing intervals and helped him learn some control as he "waited" to try again.

Between 5–6 months, much to my delight, he began to communicate with grunting. This worked well until he began to use this new form of communicating to signal for other things (i.e., to nurse, for attention or to practice newfound vocal abilities). It was at this time that I became unsure of myself and took my son more frequently than necessary to the bathroom. It is easy to misconceive that all this becomes a perfect routine, rather than a development of communication. I soon found out that other mothers went through the same thing and that the best thing to do was back off and relax. It was around this time, too, that I discovered what I call a "warning pee." I would check my son's diaper when uncertain if he had cued and find a warm, wet spot. This prompted me to take him to the bathroom where he would commence to pee a large amount, after patiently waiting for me to remove his diaper and position him. This was a fascinating development in communication during this phase of second-guessing myself. It also reconfirmed that he truly was developing control at such a young age!

Soon other cues began to emerge. Zachary was cueing visually with a beckoning or imploring look. Upon seeing "the look" and responding/taking him to the bathroom, he eliminated with success on the toilet. It was so encouraging! After beginning solids at 6 months, I also became aware that when he seemed to lose interest in eating earlier than usual, it often meant he was concentrating on "going" or was about to "go." As I continued with this method, I was becoming more in tune with him and starting to experience subtler forms of communication. It would just "hit" me that he needed to go, and then I began to connect this with what he was or was not doing at the time. How connected I felt with my son!

By 8 months I was utilizing training pants with him exclusively, without the vinyl covers. As a result, I became even more in tune with Zachary, being "forced" to focus on him and his communication. We would have 0–3 accidents a day and often go several consecutive days without any accidents. I also began to use a timer to help keep aware of when Zachary needed to pee again, based on his timing. This helped me remember when I was caught up doing other things which were distracting and making me lose focus.

Around 8 months, he started to come to me while saying "ma, ma, ma," and then would tap my leg to go potty or nurse. Then he started crawling to the bathroom when he had to go. There were times where he would drop his toys or interrupt his play to do this. If I was sitting on the floor, he would crawl to me and tap me on the leg or else crawl up onto my knees and into my lap if he had to go. At 9 months, I observed him lean towards the bathroom with his imploring look as he watched his father go there to shave.

At 9 months, he was able to patiently wait to be positioned before "going." In fact, this seemed to happen almost overnight, when the interval between potty sessions increased from 20–45 minutes to up to 2½ hours, just a week into his 9th month.

Near the end of 9 months, he began crawling to the bathroom and pulling himself up to stand at the toilet. He would even open the lid and pat the seat at times, while waiting to be positioned. Other times, he would hold my hand and we would walk to the bathroom together. Also at the end of 9 months, we began instructing him on the ASL sign for "toilet" by making the sign every time we asked if he needed to go and every time we took him to the bathroom. When he gave indication of his need to go, we again would use the sign as we took him into the bathroom. Within a week of introducing him to the sign, he was using it. He would even sign "toilet" when he heard someone else flush or when someone uttered the word "toilet." Signing was decidedly helpful in public settings such as church in that it was a subtle communication and only we were aware of why we stepped out of the service for a moment!

Nights . . .

When Zachary was about 6½ months old, I had found and read more material on this method and discovered his restlessness at night was a cue for his need to pee. If I ignored his restlessness, he would often go in his sleep. When I responded and toileted him just as I did during the day, he would pee, then return to bed asleep, no longer restless as he had been prior to being toileted. Here is how I handled nights.

Step 1 consisted of responding to Zachary's restlessness in his sleep. Whether he awoke fully or not, I took him to pee. He would often pee (or on a rare occasion, poop) on the toilet in his sleep, leaning against me with his eyes closed while he eliminated and afterwards just sigh.

For Step 2, I applied timing in addition to watching for restlessness at night. Timing helped me know when to take him to the toilet on occasions when he was in a deep sleep and didn't stir at night. The transition to training pants also eased our nighttime routine. For a while I would remove his training pants before picking him up to take him to the bathroom, to help communicate that this was why I was coming into his room when he was supposed to be going to sleep.

Step 3 happened around 8–9 months when he began to wake more and more on his own to be toileted, as opposed to my responding solely to his restlessness or timing. Upon awakening, I would hear him moving and find him up on his knees, waiting to be taken to the toilet. He seemed to connect that Mommy or Daddy would respond if he awakened to pee at night.

Step 4 happened around 9–10 months when he cried out to us, got up in his bed and waited to be toileted. From this point on, we used a combination of all four steps, and accidents soon became a thing of the past. At 9 months, he sometimes used toilet visits as a bedtime delay tactic. To accomplish this, he would cry out (or at 10 months sign), and when we got to the bathroom, he would void just a trickle of pee.

At 10 months when he awoke on his own, he would call out to us and then upon our arrival, we'd find him standing or on his knees, making the ASL toilet sign by emphatically waving his little fist.

After he weaned at 18 months, he did not awaken at night unless he had something to drink prior to bed that made him have to go at night. He continued to be reliable in waking up when he needed to go to the bathroom. Imagine having a young toddler who can drink before bedtime or in the night and still stay dry, awakening on his own to be toileted!

A Mom & Two Nannies

Sherri Tomlin is a chiropractor living in San Jose, California. Her husband, Robert Martines, is also a chiropractor. They have their own practices. Sherri first heard about infant potty training when their son Lucas was 7 months old. He is now 12½ months old. Here's what Sherri had to say in 2000.

I was in an attachment parenting playgroup and one day one of the mothers started talking about infant potty training. The first thing I thought was that the woman was crazy. She demonstrated how the method worked with her little boy, and I found it interesting. I went home and thought of all the reasons why it wouldn't work for me: because I work, because I use babysitters, because my husband might object, etc. I had lots of doubts, but this is the way I always process things, by working through my doubts.

Several days later, I woke up, went into the kitchen and got a bowl to see how it would fit Lucas. I wondered if he would accept or reject it. He was 7½ months old. I had been told that 6 months was the maximum age that I should start this, but I also had understood that it needs to be done before babies disconnect from their sense of elimination. Being a chiropractor, I understand how the nerves and the nervous system work and that it's extremely different from individual to individual, no matter what the books say or what other people's experiences are. There are always exceptions or unusual circumstances. The way I started potty training Lucas was to just test a bowl to see how it would work. The bowl was from a set of nesting plastic bowls from the kitchen. I sat him on the middle-sized bowl in my lap since that was the way my friend had held her baby and also because the bowl wasn't stable on its own. Lucas didn't object, and we just went from there.

Before we had started the potty training, Lucas used to cry frequently during the night. When I started getting up and putting him on the potty, it quieted him down. I realized his crying was his way of letting me know he didn't like to be wet, and in this way, I knew for sure that he was still connected with the sensation that he needed to go potty.

Lucas has two caregivers or babysitters. One of them is a nanny and the other is a school teacher, so they are both very experienced in working with children. One of them takes Lucas three mornings and the other takes him two afternoons, for a total of five half days a week. When I first met them, I told them about infant potty training, but they were reluctant to try it.

I knew I could do infant toilet training with or without the help of the caregivers. I understand that even tiny babies know the difference between individuals and will test different individuals in different ways. They'll do one thing with Grandma that they won't do with Mom. If the babysitters wouldn't use the method, I planned to tell Lucas, "When you're not with Mommy, just go in the diaper."

I gave a book on IPT to the caregivers. At first, they didn't want to commit to it. After some days, one of them came to me and confessed that they had been doing it for three days. They talk to each other every evening. They had been discussing it with each other and had decided to give it a try.

Lucas works well with the caregivers. I found out that their original hesitation was that they feared they wouldn't do it right. They wanted to do it perfectly. They are very proud of their success. They keep a notebook for me. Everyday I get a page of detailed notes of what went on the during the day, and this includes the potty progress. They write if he peed or pooed in the potty or if they missed getting him to the potty on time.

We used the little plastic bowl until one day someone dropped it and cracked it. Then I bought a potty. Since it had a stable base, I could let Lucas sit on the potty on the floor instead of in my lap. He had no trouble sitting on it. I kept my arms around him at first. It was like I was the one who needed to have him go through the infant process instead of him needing to do this.

Sometimes we have several perfect days in a row, and some days it is difficult. On difficult days I try to focus on not getting frustrated. I strive to just accept the frustration and feel it fully so I can let it go and move on.

Sometimes when he won't sit on the potty I take him outside and let him wander around naked. That seems to give him a little space, time to deal with things and then he goes back to the potty. It's really a dance—a pushing and pulling. Sometimes when we're dancing we step on each other's feet, but most of the time we're having fun with it.

There are three main ways that I know he needs to go potty. First, timing. A lot of it is based on timing, putting him on the potty just after a meal or when we get up in the morning. Second, communication. He signals me in different ways like

Robert Martines

Lucas takes a pee . . . in the family SUV.

grunting, crying or crawling over to get me, although sometimes he crawls to me right after he has peed in his pants; I take this to mean he is uncomfortable and wants to be changed. The third element I use is my intuition. For example, one day I was leaving the office. It was late in the day and I was just pulling out when I had a thought, "I wonder if Lucas needs to go poo? When was the last time I pooed him?" I almost did something that is typical of me, which is to say to myself, "Oh, he's fine. I'll do it when I get home." I almost drove out the driveway. That was the moment I realized, "Wait a minute. That's the little voice in me, talking to me." The more I listen to that little voice, the clearer it becomes. I backed up into the parking lot, nursed Lucas, then put him on the potty in the back of the truck, and he went. I had a successful outcome from listening to that little voice.

I think listening to that voice is important. The times that I have missed getting him to the potty on time and I feel frustrated with myself are times when I'm on the telephone, doing the laundry or driving somewhere. In other words, something is distracting me, and I'm not listening to that little voice. I have to listen to that little voice about many things, not just elimination.

This method isn't for everyone, but people should at least know it's a viable option. If it sounds right for them, they will try it. In trying, they will succeed or fail. If they succeed, great! If they fail . . . no harm done, but it's certainly worth a try!

Chapter 11
Cross-Cultural Studies

Every society has some sort of guidelines for how to handle a newborn, what precautions to take and when to expect what from baby. Different people around the world have different expectations, training methods and time frames. The age at which a mother and a society expect her baby to learn certain skills can influence the way she interacts with the baby. Expectations, training and handling of infants set the tone and pace for learning.

Most American and European parents believe that behaviors such as maintaining constant physical contact, nursing on demand and quickly responding to crying will spoil a child. In Western countries, much importance is placed upon rearing independent children.[35] In fact, the biggest difference between Western child-rearing practices and those of many other parts of the world is the amount of close, physical contact between mother and baby. In rural areas of most developing countries, infants are:

- born at home (sometimes in a clinic) via natural childbirth and immediately held by mother or caregiver
- closely bonded with their mothers during a postpartum honeymoon ("babymoon"), often in seclusion, lasting from 7 to 80 days
- in constant and close physical contact with their mother or caregiver(s) until they walk
- held or carried throughout most of the day
- kept in bed, or on a mat or cot, beside their mother all night
- nursed on demand for 1–4 years, sometimes longer
- immediately soothed and never left to cry
- never alone
- rarely disciplined or punished
- generally not diapered (except in some affluent families or when using natural materials)
- not pressured to be toilet trained

Another component of nurturant cultures is the casual and relaxed attitude towards infant elimination and toilet training. Although the odor of feces can be unpleasant, there are no hysterically negative feelings about excreta. By way of comparison, Westerners often feel that dealing with elimination is disgusting and "yucky." Some resent or punish infants for making a mess.

Since the late 20th century, more and more Western families have been adopting a number of the nurturant practices mentioned in this book—practices such as baby-wearing, family sleeping, quick response to crying and nursing on demand. At the same time, a number of families in third world countries are abandoning traditional ways and swapping some of their customs for Western ones, such as bottle-feeding, early weaning, diapers and leaving baby alone in a crib or other location—mainly in the case of affluent or well-educated families, but there are exceptions.

Three countries where IPT is still mainstream are China, India and Vietnam. Brief testimonials from all three are included below. For readers interested in learning more about cross-cultural IPT findings and testimonials, the book *Infant Potty Training* dedicates around 150 pages of text and photos to cross-cultural studies.

China

China is fairly well-known for its use of infant elimination training. This testimonial is especially interesting in that it contains reports concerning three generations of the same family—the parents in China and their daughter and grandson who live in a Western society. The first report is by Sun Mengjia and Li Minqian, retired physics professors from Shanxi University in Taiyuan, Shanxi. The second report comes from their daughter Min Sun, who holds a Ph.D. in Nutrition Sciences from the University of Alabama at Birmingham, resides in Italy and is married to an Italian pediatrician. Both reports were filed in 2002.

Sun Mengjia and Li Minqian (China)

In China, parents usually begin toilet training around the age of 1 month or as late as 4 months. Sometimes they base it on starting after the first 100 days of life since the first 100 days are important in Chinese culture. Babies are considered to be very fragile for the first 100 days. But many diligent mothers and grandmothers start training within the first month with the expectation that, according to a Chinese proverb, they "get twice the result with half the effort."

The reason for starting toilet training in infancy is to help infants build good habits. Many Chinese books on infant rearing advocate early training and include summaries of thousands of cases. There are now also some authors who follow Western beliefs and advise to begin training at age 18 months. But most parents feel that if training starts at this late time, it is very difficult because you have to correct bad habits which have already been formed.

We toilet trained our two children according to Chinese tradition. A fundamental principle is: Eating and elimination are two coexisting aspects that should be considered equally important. We learned the timing and regularity of our babies' eliminations, based on their feeding schedule. At the most likely time for the babies to eliminate, we held them in a specific position and guided them with sounds. For the infant elimination position, the baby rests his back against the mother's chest and the mother holds the baby's legs in her hands. In Chinese, to *ba* a baby means to help a baby eliminate (*ba* is a verb in the third tone). A typical sound for voiding is *xu* and for defecation *eng* is often used. These are used to help the infant develop the ability to control elimination, by building a healthy conditioned reflex.

Chinese books on child rearing state that babies can recognize the *ba* position with sounds as early as 20–30 days old; this combination can help them accomplish early training. In China, we are proud when our children are trained early. Toilet training is usually completed between 4–12 months.

Parents have help with toilet training. Usually the grandparents assist, but if not, a full-time babysitter or helper (who sometimes stays with the family) is hired to follow the mother's instructions. Open pants are used for convenience and timeliness of elimination, before good control is gained.

Valdin/Photononstop

An Ouighour baby in split pants.
Grandfather and grandson "hanging out" together.
(Xinjiang, China)

Ivy Makelin

Open Pants.
Split pants are used
throughout much
of China.

It is fairly common to see
a large opening with a baby
butt hanging out of split pants
in China. There is no shame,
shock or moral judgment
upon seeing a baby bottom
in China. And for those who
prefer it, less open styles are
readily available.

With smaller infants, a cotton
cloth or towel is sometimes
used in case of accidents.
The cloth is slipped under
the waistband or else held
in place by the caregiver
or a cotton tie.

Open Pants.
This style of pants has a very
small opening.

Ivy Makelin

In China, infants sleep next to their parents, so babies feel safe. In this way, an attentive mother can feel or observe the movements of her baby. During the night, if a baby moves or wakes up for elimination needs, the mother will *ba* her baby to urinate.

Sun Min (Italy)

I think that infant toilet training is a learning process for me as a mother but not a training process for my baby because I am not training him but only learning the timing and communications for his elimination needs. I am helping him build a healthy habit from early infancy. When our son was born, my parents sent information from China on the importance and how-tos of infant toilet training. I discussed it with my husband. He, as an Italian pediatrician and neonatologist, had never heard about this. Initially he was surprised, but eventually he told me that I could try anything with our baby. So I started toilet training with a way that suited our lifestyle in Italy—I started early, did not use Chinese open pants but used disposable diapers for a while.

A lot of people, whether they are mothers or not, can tell when a baby needs to go, but they have never considered taking the baby to the bathroom for this. When our baby was 1 month old, I thought, if I know my baby is going to make stools, why don't I take him to the bathroom instead of watching him make it in the diaper—it's better to bring him to the bathroom and wash him in the same position. The process began with a thought as easy as this.

By 4 months of age, I was able to help him defecate in the bathroom. By 7 months, he stayed dry during day naps. Now he is 9 months old and jumps up and down in front of the potty!

When he goes for me in the bathroom, I praise him and give him a little kiss. When accidents occur, I blame myself for not being able to pay enough attention to catch his signals. Now that he is 9 months old, I don't need to observe him so closely anymore. I simply take him to the bathroom when I feel it is the right time. I do think he has learned to cooperate with me in that he sometimes waits by holding it before I take him to the bathroom.

My philosophy is that everything has to be moderate, and we should not abuse our resources. Diapers can be used before baby gains full control, but learning how our babies communicate their needs is also important and particularly interesting. If they cry due to hunger, feeling ignored or being sleepy or tired, it makes sense that they also cry for other reasons, which include their elimination needs. Babies communicate with us before they can speak. If we don't understand, it is because we don't listen with attentive hearts. If we help our babies eat, dress and wash before they can do these things by themselves, why can't we bring them to the bathroom before they can do this by themselves? Parents should be educated to help children build healthy elimination habits starting at birth, then teach them independent toileting later. This is a civilized and educated way to bring up our babies. We should inform all parents about this possibility, so they can choose whether to start early or at 2 years of age.

India

Neelam and Raj Mehta raised two children in Gujarat, India, using infant potty training. Their daughter Sheil started at 4 months and completed potty training at 13 months while their son Yash took about two months longer to train than his sister. Here is what Neelam had to say in 2000 on the topic of toilet training her children in the state of Gujarat.

My husband Raj helped me quite a bit with toilet training. We lived with our extended family so I also had a lot of help from my relatives in the home. In India, we nurse our babies, then get a feel for how long after a feeding baby needs to go to the bathroom. Mothers intuitively know when it is time to take baby to the bathroom. It doesn't take long to learn this. The feeling is based in part on timing but not on watching a clock. It is a matter of realizing it is time.

The closest thing to a diaper that we use is a little cotton garment called a *balotu*. It resembles a G-string or skimpy underwear. This infant underwear is more comfortable and functional than a bulky towel between the legs, which is how Western diapers appear to us. We use the little underwear on infants before we start toilet training and also in the beginning stages of training, in between visits to the bathroom. Once our babies head to the bathroom on their own, we let them wear regular children's underpants.

Bathrooms in India are simple and small. Ours was smaller than four feet by four feet. Indian bathrooms typically consist of a tile or cement floor. We don't have plumbing fixtures like a tub, sink or toilet. Instead, we just squat down and go on the floor. There is always a bucket full of water and a bar of soap in the bathroom. We rinse the floor and clean ourselves. This may sound unhygienic to people in the West, but our bathrooms are very clean.

When we want an infant to pee, we start by making the sound "sssss," which sounds like water. After a while, we just tell them to "go pee pee." We don't make a special noise for them to poop.

When babies are really small, there are two things we do to keep them clean. One is to have them lying on a blanket or soft cloth on a cot (bed). When it's time to poop, we gently grasp and raise the baby's ankles in order to lift his buttocks off the blanket while he is pooping. This way he doesn't get soiled. We replace the cloth under him with a clean one, then lay him down again. Another way we take small babies to poop is by cradling or holding them in our arms while they eliminate.

I started toilet training my daughter Sheil when she was 4 months old. I would nurse Sheil, then take her to pee about an hour later and then take her at regular intervals after that. I would take her to the bathroom, remove her underwear, make the "sssss" sound and remain in the bathroom with her until she went. I held her in my arms, supported her head and squatted or sat while I waited for her to go. Within a few weeks, the time between pees increased, so I would take her every hour and a half. Then it increased to every two hours. She almost finished with bowel training by 6 months. She understood that when I took her to the bathroom and removed her infant underwear, it meant she should poop or pee. Around 6 months, I believe Sheil really understood toilet training. She sensed why I took her to the bathroom and what she should do there. I stopped using infant underwear with her at this stage and used panties instead.

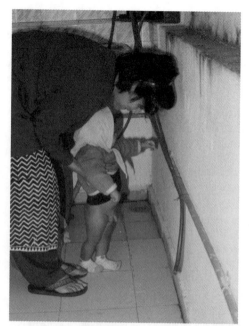

Pathak

**Mother supports 12-month-old as he pees
in typical Indian bathroom (Gujarat, India).**

Sheil also started crawling around 6 months. She would crawl to the bathroom door, remain there, look at me and make sounds to get my attention. I understood that she was calling me and letting me know she had to go to the bathroom. She would remain by the bathroom door until I arrived to take her to the toilet. As soon as I took her in the bathroom and removed her panties, she would pee.

At 9 months she walked well on her own and would say "Mommy bathroom, Mommy bathroom" when she had to go. I considered her toilet trained at 9 months, even though she still needed my help to get into the bathroom and pull down her panties. She was completely toilet trained, able to do everything independently, at age 13 months.

I started toilet training my son Yash when he was 3 months old. From the age of 3 months, he never wet the bed at night, whereas his sister sometimes wet the bed until the age of 4½ months. But for the rest of the potty process, it took my son longer than his sister to learn.

He started to crawl around 4 months but didn't head for the bathroom door on his own until a few months later. It was harder for me to know when he had to pee than it was with his sister. He would pee more often, so it took more time than I spent working with his sister to keep him dry.

At 8 months, he started crawling to the bathroom door when he had to go. At this point, he started wearing underpants. He walked and had good control over elimination at 12 months. In fact, he would always hold it until I arrived to take him in the bathroom. He didn't start talking for another half year, so instead he would

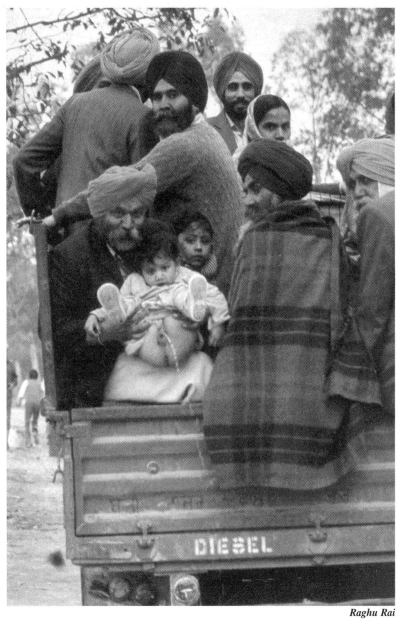

Raghu Rai

Improvising a "toilet place" on the road during a Sikh outing (1982).

use his own sign language to tell me things. He had ways to sign to me if he wanted to pee or poop. I considered him toilet trained at 12 months of age, but he still needed help with his clothing at that age.

Yash was 1½ years old when we left India for the United States. He was almost finished with toilet training at that time so I never used a diaper on him in this country.

Children learn things at an early age in India. This is partly due to living with an extended family where there are always at least eight people living in a house. Children are never alone. There are always two or more people with them. They hear people talking all the time. We talk to our children a lot, and they learn very quickly this way.

In the past, this method of toilet training from birth was used throughout India. Nowadays, I'd say it is used in about 85% of the country. This is because many women now have jobs. In cities, up to 50% of women work and don't have time to raise their kids like we traditionally raise them. The women in cities like to be modern and use the Western-style toilet training with diapers. Married couples don't want to have to deal with the rest of the extended family. This means mothers in cities don't have help from the extended family and are using diapers to delay potty training. In villages, families still live together and use the traditional and natural means of toilet training.

Toilet training doesn't stress or frustrate people in India. We don't view it as time consuming or a chore like Westerners do. It's just a natural thing, something you do for your baby, part of your duties to raise a child.

If I had another child while living in the United States, I would still start toilet training in infancy, the same as I did for my other two children. I could not do it on my own since my husband and I own and operate a shop. I would send for my extended family and bring them over from India to be with me and the baby.

Vietnam

Randy Mont-Reynaud raised three children using infant potty training from birth. She holds a Ph.D. in Developmental Psychology from Harvard University. She studied with Jerome Kagan and conducted research for her dissertation on emotional and cognitive development among Vietnamese infants in the second year of life. She is currently at Stanford University.

Dr. Mont-Reynaud went to Vietnam in 1967 to study child development. She lived in Saigon for six months, attained a modest level of competence in speaking Vietnamese, then returned to the United States and obtained her master's degree in anthropology. In 1972 she returned to Vietnam and spent two years studying child development and religious beliefs in a village setting. She took up residence in the village of My Duc, some miles from the Cambodian border, in the province of Chau Doc. She adopted her first child while residing in the village—and thus learned about child rearing firsthand. Her son was rarely in diapers in Vietnam and comfortably (i.e., without stress) made the transition to proper toilet behavior by the age of 18 months when he accompanied Dr. Mont-Reynaud back to the USA.

Dr. Mont-Reynaud raised two more children, a son and a daughter, in the USA. Like their older brother, they were kept out of diapers as much as possible and comfortably transitioned to standard toilet behavior. Her report was written in 2000.

In Vietnam, where I learned about infant care and toileting, infants and toddlers are held off the porch or at arm's distance of a lap or taken outside to "go." I call the process "mother training" or "caregiver training" because what it really relies on is the mother or caregiver being responsive to the infant's cues and getting the child to the proper place/location. "Misses," in the form of caregivers failing to carry babies to the proper place at the right time, are occasions for laughter . . . and that's all.

The process starts with a newborn. First, you observe when your infant pees or poos and make a little whispering noise at that instant—or soon after. It appears that infants quickly recognize that when they relieve themselves this way, they also hear the whispering noise. Second, make the whispering noise when you know your baby is about to pee or poop. The baby will respond to your cue and "go" for you. It's Skinnerian, basic behaviorist psychology. It is undergirded by the simple fact that newborns pee and poop all the time. It all boils down to training children to respond to stimuli. It's hard to miss, especially if babies are not diapered and you are holding them. Then soon whenever they hear the noise, they will respond if they need to eliminate. The important thing to remember is that it works if they need to go—"if" being the operative word here. Obviously, if you don't have to go, you don't have to go.

It doesn't take long before an infant (around 1 month old) understands what you are doing. I say "understand," because you're not sitting down and explaining to the baby, "Whenever I do this, this is what you'll do." It's an association of feeling states. The baby is first feeling a sensation, feeling that he is peeing or pooing, then hearing your cue. Within a week, you can make the little whispering noise and the baby will pee or poo on demand (providing s/he needs to eliminate at that time).

If you don't have any help, the process is fairly labor intensive in the beginning. After labor and delivery, you may not feel like paying attention to this all the time. Sometimes you'll be too tired, busy or breastfeeding. At times it is hit or miss. If you make a good effort, it won't harm a child if you aren't there for every pee or poo. Babies still get it. You can't do it round the clock every single day. If you sometimes don't get to do it or forget, it's not crucial. The important thing to note here is that in the village, folks are not establishing correct toilet behavior as a goal at this stage (or later). This is just how they handle the situation until the child understands and is physically able to walk to the proper place.

Don't fasten a diaper around a tiny infant. It's better to place the infant on a diaper, but don't enclose the baby in the diaper in the traditional fashion. When you're nursing your baby, if the child is wrapped loosely in a towel or diaper, you'll know instantly when your child pees or poops.

How do you know when your baby needs to go? I asked this question in the Vietnamese village. The women looked at me and said, "Well, how do you know when you need to go?" This tipped me off to understanding the connection between toilet learning and the mother-child bond or the caregiver-infant bond. They are a very close unit. You come to know when your baby has to pee/relieve himself (same as we "know"—or think we know—when a child is hungry or tired. You just "know"!). Most mothers/caregivers (this could be a grandmother, sister or aunt) who are involved, in tune and bonded with their baby know when a baby is hungry or tired. Parents attribute some feeling state to a crying baby. The attribution may or may not be correct at first, but eventually over a short period of time it becomes correct as you get to know your baby.

It helps if you can keep your child bare-bottomed. Of course this is easier in warm climates like in California or Hawaii, but you can do it elsewhere if you want. This method eliminates the diaper rash problem, and it's about keeping a baby clean. The bottom line for potty training is this: If you do not want your child to poop in a diaper, take the diaper off!

When babies start crawling or walking, keep a little potty where they can see it. It's amazing, they just go there and do it. By the time babies can walk, they get where they need to go if they have observed that behavior. Around 15 months or so, kids begin to understand there is a standard. They understand they are supposed to be somewhere to go potty, that there is a place (i.e., potty) to pee and the rest of the world is not where you pee.

The Vietnamese regard mother training as a natural process. They don't expect children to have difficulties with it—and babies don't. The Vietnamese don't expect it to be problematic for the mother, and it isn't, although there are occasional "slipups." Mother training is something everyone accepts and expects, like breathing. No one teaches us to breathe, but we all do it. Mother training is not something that is learned. It is just something babies do from the moment they are born. They conform to a behavior. By comparison, people in Western cultures have made potty training into an unnatural act and an ordeal.

It is the mother who is primarily responsible for what Westerners call potty training. You might think that the mother never gets a break, but in Vietnam, the baby may be passed around to a whole cadre of siblings and extended relatives or just other folks.

In the villages, mothers don't use a potty, and traditionally there are no diapers. They sometimes wrap a towel around the baby on their lap. If the baby needs to pee, the women just hold the infant facing away from them, either on their lap or at the edge of the porch. The baby quickly comprehends, "I move through space to do this elsewhere."

There are usually no toilets in Vietnamese villages. In the rare situations where there is a toilet, it's a Turkish toilet that you squat to use. Obviously an infant can't squat. The mother goes to the area, squats down, holds the baby with legs spread apart and the baby goes. So you bring the child to a part of the house, or a place outside the house, where it is to go. It's not very far to take the baby.

Of course this is not a perfect system, and accidents do happen. The Vietnamese attitude towards accidents is very casual—elimination is just a normal thing, this is what babies do and when necessary, you clean it up. If a baby is starting to pee and he's on your lap, you just hold him over the porch to go, or you mop up the spill from the tile floor. If it's a dirt floor, you don't have to worry about it. In our culture there are other things to worry about like carpets and expensive clothing.

I adopted my first child in Vietnam when he was 4 months old and began mother training immediately. The Vietnamese taught me a simple form of body language that baby boys exhibit when they have to pee. You know a boy needs to pee when you see his penis wiggle. This of course assumes someone is watching a baby boy's penis, which in our culture is a no-no. We don't look at genitals here, but in Vietnam, they do so without impunity. They know that a penis wiggles just before a baby boy has to pee. I'll bet mothers in this country don't know this because we have been bundling babies and toddlers up all these years.

By the time my baby was able to sit up, I could place him on a pot if I had one nearby. When he started walking at 10 months, he had a regular, once-a-day routine for poop. By age 1 year, he was regular like a clock. By the time children walk, they know what the elimination standard is and where they are supposed to be with it.

After spending a year in the village, we moved to Israel where we spent six months, then we moved to Vermont. I later had two birth children, a boy and a girl. It was a lot of fun trying to implement mother training with them from birth. I was 35 and living in California when my son was born. It might have been easier if I was younger. Between nursing and caring for an older child, an 18-hour labor and experiencing my first birth, it was a lot to handle.

There was a huge wall-to-wall mirror over the bathroom sink in our home. When I held him over the sink, he could see himself in the mirror and could see me holding him. When he peed or pooed, of course I was happy and would smile. (In Vietnam they don't smile and don't praise a child for peeing. Why should they?) I was thrilled to see him respond to my cue. He could see in the mirror that I was happy with his behavior. Then he would smile and see his reflection in the mirror, and that would reward him even more.

The second child I gave birth to was a daughter. I started mother training her at birth. I was living in California. Her little brother was 26 months when she was born. She observed him using a potty and seemed to want to imitate him. This is another thing I had studied at Harvard—imitation and modeling. Children want to be like the model. If they see a model doing something, they want to do it too. Monkey see, monkey do. In our culture, children don't commonly see adults on the toilet. We close the bathroom door. A lot of mothers won't even let their children in the bathroom with them, and this is one reason why traditional toilet training takes so long.

My daughter was able to sit on a pot by 6 months. When children need to go, they see the potty and take care of business. Both these children could do this sometime between 6 and 8 months. They would crawl towards the potty on the carpeted floor in the living room. I would see them making their way across the room and sit them on the potty. If you expose children to the stimulus-response behavior in infancy and let them know what the expectation is, it's amazing how fast they catch on. By 6 months, babies understand that a potty is where they have to go. At 18 months, all my children were able to get to a potty by themselves and could therefore be without diapers. They were actually able to be without diapers much younger than 18 months, but there were no mistakes or accidents after 18 months. Needless to say, you have to be pretty attentive, as a parent, to facilitate this in a Western non-village setting—with carpets, no less!

We hold certain beliefs most dear to us in the United States, and in our belief system, children belong in diapers. If you challenge this notion, you run the risk of being ridiculed. To parents and so-called experts who object to raising babies without diapers: If you don't want to do it, don't do it. Save your carpets!

In Vietnam and other village cultures, toddlers see the consequences of their actions in regard to toilet behavior. It's time to look at what we left behind when we left village life, look at what other cultures have to offer and, without preconceived notions, glean the gems from other cultures. We can't adopt all their customs or import them like soy sauce or tofu, but many customs are worthy of reflection.

Chapter 12
Onward

This chapter provides information and resources for further learning, support and research.

Countries Where IPT Is Practiced

Below is a list of some of the countries where IPT is practiced, based upon research to date. In some countries, it is the mainstream method, while in others it is used by a minority of families. This list is by no means exhaustive. Readers who have experienced IPT in other countries are welcome to contact the publisher with details, with a view to adding more countries to this list in future editions. For readers interested in learning about other societies using infant elimination training, the book *Infant Potty Training* contains testimonials, anthropological reports and historical references from some of these countries and peoples, as well as from the Apache, Hopi, Navaho and Papago Indians.

Africa
Algeria, Botswana, Cameroon, Central African Republic, Egypt, Ethiopia, Ghana, Ivory Coast, Kenya, Madagascar, Mali, Nigeria, Senegal, South Africa, Sudan, Tanzania, Togo, Uganda, West Africa, Zaire

Asia
Afghanistan, Bangladesh, China, French Polynesia, India, Indonesia, Iran, Iraq, Japan, Kazakhstan, Korea, Kurdistan, Lebanon, Malaysia, Micronesia, Myanmar (Burma), New Guinea, Oman, Pakistan, Peru, Philippines, Russia, Sikkim, Sri Lanka, Taiwan, Thailand, Tibet, Turkey, Vietnam

Central & South America and Caribbean
Argentina, Belize, Bolivia, Brazil, Dominican Republic, Jamaica, Mexico, Paraguay, Venezuela, West Indies

Polar Regions
Alaska (Inupiat, Eskimos), Aleutians, Canada (Inuit, Kwakiutl, Netsilik and Utkuhikhalingmiut), Greenland, Siberia

Europe
Bulgaria, Czechoslovakia, Romania, Russia, Turkey

If you have the opportunity to travel to one or more of these countries, keep your eyes open for mothers peeing their babies, and don't hesitate to strike up a conversation or show interest. Bear in mind that there is no special term for IPT abroad since it is simply the way things are done by many women. Even if you can't speak each other's languages, it is possible to communicate with gestures, smiles and body language.

Support for Infant Pottying

There are many ways to combat resistance, skepticism and negativity about IPT. If it's time to take your baby to go and you'd rather not deal with anyone's disapproval, just announce that it's time to change your baby, head for the bathroom and potty your baby in privacy.

But sometimes seeing is believing. If you can get your spouse or parents to witness IPT in action, this could be enough to cause a change of heart on their part.

Experiencing is believing too. Let a doubting husband or grandmother potty your baby at an optimum time. Once they personally get baby to go for them on one or more occasions, they might well open up to the concept and practice.

Choose a supportive pediatrician. Many Western pediatricians are not familiar with IPT, but there are some who have had personal experience with the method, and others may surprise you once your baby surprises them.

Join or start an infant potty playgroup with like-minded parents. It is encouraging, educational and fun to share your experiences and insights. Invite guest speakers, such as parents of IPT graduates. Getting together with others helps alleviate feelings of isolation, of being misunderstood and an outsider, and also reaffirms your beliefs.

Talk to friends and immigrants with a background in infant elimination training. Most are delighted to offer advice and support. If you are a member of an IPT playgroup, invite experienced immigrants to join the group or attend a session.

Visit or join helpful websites, e-mail lists and bulletin boards. The Infant Potty Training Homepage (http://www.timl.com/ipt) leads to many articles and related sites. Since website addresses change or become outdated so often, no others are listed here. Another way to access online information is to use an Internet search engine to conduct searches for some of the terms coined by different mothers who have discovered this method on their own—terms such as "infant potty training," "elimination communication," "babies without diapers," "diaperless" and "diaper free." And there are websites in other languages, including German, Italian, Swedish, French and Hebrew.

Learn from books, articles and videos. Ask your librarian to help you find more material. The following is a list of dedicated book and video material available in or through many libraries at the time of printing:

- *Infant Potty Basics: With or Without Diapers . . . the Natural Way*, Laurie Boucke, White-Boucke Publishing, 110 pages, 2003.
- *Infant Potty Training: A Gentle and Primeval Method Adapted to Modern Living*, Laurie Boucke, White-Boucke Publishing, 500 pages, 2002.
- *The Potty Project*, Dr. Barbara Gablehouse, Five Star Parenting, VHS video, 2000.
- *Diaper Free! The Gentle Wisdom of Natural Infant Hygiene*, Ingrid Bauer, Natural Wisdom Press, 250 pages, 2000.
- *Infant Communication: Raising Babies Without Diapers . . . and More*, Natec, Children's Liberation Front, 25 pages, 1990-2001.
- *Trickle Treat: Diaperless Infant Toilet Training Method*, Laurie Boucke, White-Boucke Publishing, 87 pages, 1991.

All of these resources except *Trickle Treat* are currently in print and available for purchase via the Internet or special order from bookstores or the publishers.

It is also important to build support from within, on all levels—physical, mental and emotional. All mothers feel overwhelmed and exhausted at times. Don't let days like these affect your long-term desires. If you are heading towards or experiencing burnout or depression, immediately shift gears and attitude. Take comfort in knowing that the trying times will pass and that soon you will regain your strength and enthusiasm.

Improve your lifestyle. Participate in a physical activity that you love, such as walking, hiking, swimming or biking, at least a few days a week. Listen to your favorite music. Find time to deeply relax. Make it a priority to rest or take "power naps" more often. Simplify your life. Reconsider your priorities. Cut out unnecessary tasks. Use diapers as a backup. If helpful, take a break from pottying for some hours or days.

Never forget that it is normal to have accidents. Don't beat up on yourself or feel any guilt about accidents or a few bad days or weeks. Always remember that there will be an ebb and flow of developmental progress, with 1–2 steps back for every 3 steps forward. Avoid comparing your baby with any other. Respect her natural rate of development.

If you're feeling confused or having doubts, reevaluate your situation and outlook. Don't let societal pressures or your past dictate or limit your behavior and aspirations. Free yourself of unrealistic expectations about IPT. Remember: no perfectionism, and no competition with other babies or parents! Don't be attached to a particular timetable or course of events. If you're trying too hard, let go and take a more laid-back approach. The benefits of infant pottying reach far beyond finishing toilet teaching at a particular time. By starting early in life, the emphasis is more on communication and bonding than on actual bladder and bowel control. The latter will come later and as a natural consequence of your being present for and responsive to your baby's elimination needs.

Work as a loving team and trust your infant's signals, rather than feel you need to be in total control by calling all the shots. Find joy in the little things and in knowing your baby is content. Remind yourself that these are precious times to be savored and enjoyed to the fullest. Give yourself credit for being a wonderful mother.

Onward

This book is a good-faith attempt to present what I believe is a correct rendition of a behavior and practice that has remained obscure in the West. The book does not claim to present scientific data. Since no scientific or academic scales or other means of measurement and testing exist, there is no way to reach a scientifically sound conclusion, but this does not mean that a general conclusion and impression about the efficacy of the method cannot be reached. The practices, preferences, cultural tendencies and claims of a number of peoples described in this book all lead to the conclusion that infant elimination training is not only possible and practiced in many societies, but it is also gentle and effective.

Ethnopediatrics is a relatively new branch of research, dating from 1995. The science focuses on the study of parenting practices used in different cultures and the effects of these practices on the health, well-being and survival of infants. The major contributors are pediatricians, anthropologists and child development researchers. The ethnopediatrician can provide valuable information and reassurance to parents who are uncertain of their parenting skills.[36] The big question at this point is whether or not ethnopediatrics will embrace and encourage infant elimination training practices. I believe it is imperative for this aspect of infant care to be included. In this regard, perhaps ethnopediatrics will one day lead to the sanctioning of an official study in order to finally give this method a fair assessment.

In the meantime, since there has not been much academic attention paid to infant elimination training, and since there is such a stigma against it in Western countries, it is hoped that the guidelines, testimonials and research provided in this book will inspire Western families interested in this method to give it a try. Your baby is ready if you are.

Notes

1. Volterra & Erting, 1990.
2. Sonna, 2003.
3. Sonna, 2003.
4. deVries & deVries, 1977.
5. Ainsworth, 1967.
6. Geber, 1998.
7. Ball, 1971.
8. Gersch, 1978.
9. Ravindranathan, 1978.
10. Smeets et al., 1985.
11. Fischer, 1990.
12. Lamb, interview with author, 1993, & e-mail to author, 1999.
13. Schaefer & DiGeronimo, 1997.
14. Altemeier & Hemme, 1999.
15. Bakker & Wyndaele, 2000.
16. Nandyal, 2000.
17. Gablehouse, 2000.
18. Sonna, e-mail to the author, 2002.
19. Rugolotto, e-mail to the author, 2002.
20. Van Pelt, 1996.
21. Nathanson, 2002.
22. MacEachern, 1990.
23. Lamb, 1990.
24. Vallely, 1990.
25. MacEachern, 1990.
26. Richer, 1999.
27. Brecevic, 1998.
28. Vallely, 1990.
29. Stortenbeek, letter to the author, 1991.
30. Vallely, 1990.
31. Vallely, 1990.
32. Brecevic, 1998.
33. Milder, 1997.
34. Greene, 1999.
35. LeVine, 1980, referenced from Fantini & Cárdenas, 1980.
36. Small, 1998.

Bibliography

Ainsworth, Mary D. Salter. *Infancy in Uganda*, Johns Hopkins Press, pp. 77–78, 83–84, 1967.

Altemeier, William A. III, and Cheryl Hemme. "The Importance of Successful Passage," *Pediatric Annals* 28:5, 276-278, May 1999.

Bakker, E. and J. J. Wyndaele. "Changes in the Toilet Training of Children during the Last 60 Years: The Cause of an Increase in Lower Urinary Tract Dysfunction?" *British Journal of Urology International* 86:248–252, 2000.

Ball, Thomas S. "Toilet Training an Infant Mongoloid at the Breast," *California Mental Health Digest* 9:80–85, 1971.

Boucke, Laurie. *Infant Potty Training: A Gentle and Primeval Method Adapted to Modern Living*, White-Boucke Publishing, 2002.

_____. *Trickle Treat: Diaperless Infant Toilet Training Method*, White-Boucke Publishing, 1991.

Brecevic, Candace. "The Diaper Debate," http://www.diaperingdecisions.com, 1998.

deVries, Marten W., and Rachel M. deVries. "Cultural Relativity of Toilet Training Readiness: A Perspective from East Africa," *Pediatrics* 60:170–177, 1977.

Fantini, Mario D., and René Cárdenas, eds. *Parenting in a Multicultural Society*, Longman, 1980.

Fischer, Paul. Letters to the Editor, "Early Toilet Training," *The Journal of Family Practice* 30:262, 1990.

Gablehouse, Barbara. *The Potty Project*, Five Star Parenting, 2000.

Geber, Marcelle. *L'enfant africain dans un monde en changement, Étude ethnopsychologique dans huit pays sud-africains*, Presses Universitaires de France, 1998.

Gersch, Marvin J. Letter to the Editor, "Early Toilet Training," *Pediatrics* 61:674, 1978.

Greene, Alan. Re: diaper rash. In Carlos E. Richer, "I have been told that cloth diapers are better for the skin of my baby . . .?". http://www.giga.com/~cricher/FAQ.htm, 1999.

Lamb, Jan Leah. Interview with the author, June 1993 and e-mail to the author re: infant potty training, Nov.–Dec. 1999.

Lamb, Marjorie. *Two Minutes a Day for Greener Planet: Quick and Simple Things You Can Do to Save Our Earth*, Harper Paperbacks, 1990.

LeVine, Robert A. "A Cross-Cultural Perspective on Parenting." In Mario D. Fantini and René Cárdenas, eds., *Parenting in a Multicultural Society*, Longman, 1980.

MacEachern, Diane. *Save Our Planet: 750 Everyday Ways You Can Help Clean up the Earth*, Dell Trade Paperback, 1990.

Milder, John. "Choosing Diapers," National Association of Diaper Services, http://www.diapernet.com/choose.htm, 1997.

Montessori, Maria. *The Secret of Childhood*, Fides, 1966.

Nathanson, Laura. "Doctor on Call: Baby Pee Problems," *Parents*, p. 107, October 2002.

Ravindranathan, S. Letter to the Editor, "Early Toilet Training," *Pediatrics* 61:674, 1978.

Richer, Carlos E. http://www.giga.com/~cricher/FAQ.htm, 1999.

Rugolotto, Simone. E-mail to the author re: infant potty training, Apr. 2002.

Schaefer, Charles E., and Theresa Foy DiGeronimo. *Toilet Training without Tears*, Signet, 1997.

Sears, William. "Toilet-Training: Tips to Tell Potty Times," http://www.AskDrSears.com, 2001.

Small, Meredith F. *Our Babies, Ourselves*, Doubleday, 1998.

Smeets, Paul M., Giulio E. Lancioni, Thomas S. Ball and Dorette S. Oliva. "Shaping Self-initiated Toileting in Infants," *Journal of Applied Behavior Analysis* 18:303–308, 1985.

Sonna, Linda. *The Everything Potty Training Book*, Adams Media, 2003 (pre-release copy).

_____. E-mail to the author re: infant potty training, Feb.–Apr. 2002.

Stortenbeek, Willem. Correspondence with the author re: diseases spread via diaper waste in landfills, Nov. 1991.

Vallely, Bernadette. *1001 Ways to Save the Planet*, Ivy Books, 1990.

Van Pelt, Katie. *Potty Training Your Baby*, Avery, 1996.

Volterra, V., and C. J. Erting, eds. *From Gesture to Language in Hearing and Deaf Children*, Springer-Verlag, 1990.

WANT MORE?

Read a much longer version of this book

Infant Potty Training: A Gentle and Primeval Method Adapted to Modern Living
ISBN 1-888580-24-0, second edition
500 pages, $19.50

Many of the chapters contain supplemental information, photos and sketches, and there are several additional chapters such as "Stage by Stage," "Part-Time Pottying" and "History & Theories." The book also includes 26 testimonials (each with its own chapter), a section dedicated to cross-cultural studies and an index.

White-Boucke Publishing, Inc.
P.O. Box 400
Lafayette CO 80026
(800) 382-7922
www.white-boucke.com